# Say the Right Thing

# Say the Right Thing

## How to Talk About Identity, Diversity, and Justice

**KENJI YOSHINO** AND

**DAVID GLASGOW**

**ATRIA** BOOKS

NEW YORK   LONDON   TORONTO   SYDNEY   NEW DELHI

**ATRIA**
BOOKS

An Imprint of Simon & Schuster, Inc.
1230 Avenue of the Americas
New York, NY 10020

First Atria Books hardcover edition February 2023

**ATRIA** BOOKS and colophon are trademarks of Simon & Schuster, Inc.

For information about special discounts for bulk purchases, please contact Simon & Schuster Special Sales at 1-866-506-1949 or business@simonandschuster.com.

The Simon & Schuster Speakers Bureau can bring authors to your live event. For more information or to book an event, contact the Simon & Schuster Speakers Bureau at 1-866-248-3049 or visit our website at www.simonspeakers.com.

Interior design by Dana Sloan

Manufactured in the United States of America

1 3 5 7 9 10 8 6 4 2

Library of Congress Cataloging-in-Publication Data
Names: Yoshino, Kenji, author.
Title: Say the right thing : how to talk about identity, diversity, and justice / Kenji Yoshino and David Glasgow.
Description: First Atria Books hardcover edition. | New York, NY : Atria Books, [2023] | Includes bibliographical references and index.
Identifiers: LCCN 2022041564 (print) | LCCN 2022041565 (ebook) | ISBN 9781982181383 (hardcover) | ISBN 9781982181406 (ebook)
Subjects: LCSH: Gender identity. | Social justice. | Social integration. | Conversation.
Classification: LCC HQ18.55 .Y67 2023 (print) | LCC HQ18.55 (ebook) | DDC 305.3—dc23/eng/20221018
LC record available at https://lccn.loc.gov/2022041564
LC ebook record available at https://lccn.loc.gov/2022041565

ISBN 978-1-9821-8138-3
ISBN 978-1-9821-8140-6 (ebook)

*For Ron, Sophia, and Luke*
*(KY)*

*For Andrew, Hugo, and Theodore*
*(DG)*

# Contents

| | | |
|---|---|---:|
| | Authors' Note | ix |
| Introduction: | **The Impossible Conversations** | 1 |
| Principle 1: | **Beware the Four Conversational Traps** | 15 |
| Principle 2: | **Build Resilience** | 35 |
| Principle 3: | **Cultivate Curiosity** | 61 |
| Principle 4: | **Disagree Respectfully** | 83 |
| Principle 5: | **Apologize Authentically** | 105 |
| Principle 6: | **Apply the Platinum Rule** | 127 |
| Principle 7: | **Be Generous to the Source** | 151 |
| Conclusion: | **The Essential Conversations** | 173 |
| | Acknowledgments | 179 |
| | Notes | 185 |
| | Index | 215 |
| | About the Authors | 223 |
| | Reading Group Guide | 225 |

# Authors' Note

This book is a work of nonfiction. Certain names and characteristics have been changed. For ease of reading, we also used the pronouns "we," "us," and "our" to describe experiences we've had either individually or together in our professional capacities at the Meltzer Center for Diversity, Inclusion, and Belonging.

# Introduction:

## The Impossible Conversations

This book is about how to have better conversations about the social identities we all hold. While we teach people to talk across their differences in our professional lives, the roots of this project are deeply personal.

We are both gay men who spent our formative years in the closet. During that time, we were desperate to talk about our own identities, but the words felt unspeakable, even to the people who mattered most in our lives. That suffocating silence led us to search for a more powerful way of communicating—one where we could speak and expect to be heard. Perhaps unsurprisingly, we both became lawyers.

Compared to the silence of our youth, the law felt wonderfully loud. It could settle disputes, compensate the injured, and fix systemic problems for millions of people. It seemed like the form of conversation that could most tangibly address injustice not just for LGBTQ+ individuals but for all outsiders who struggle to be heard.

Over time, however, living in the law showed us its limitations. Law can lay the foundation of an inclusive society, such as by banning racial discrimination in housing or by mandating equal pay for women. But bias occurs in interactions so infinite and infinitesimal that the law will never reach them all. Every day, students of color challenge prejudice in the classroom, women disclose experiences of sexual harassment, employees with disabilities ask their bosses for accommodations, and transgender teens come out to their families. We know firsthand that for vulnerable people, such interactions can be devastating when handled poorly, and transformative when handled well. Importantly, these conversations will keep happening whether the laws on the books are strong or weak.

This realization led us into diversity and inclusion—a field dedicated to helping individuals and organizations build cultures where everyone has a sense of belonging. We still take pride in being lawyers and continue to advocate for legal reforms, as we believe the law is an indispensable tool for securing basic rights. But we also want to do the work that law can't do on its own. Together, we founded the Meltzer Center for Diversity, Inclusion, and Belonging at NYU School of Law. Teaching people to have better conversations about identity, diversity, and justice is a critical part of our center's mission.

As we reflect on our young adulthood, we still remember every single one of the conversations where we came out as gay to the people we loved. Today, we often find ourselves on the other side of these critical conversations—as the people seeking to offer support rather than to receive it. Knowing the stakes of these interactions, we try to be good allies to women, transgender individuals, people with disabilities, people of color, and others who come to us. Our own failures in these current conversations have given us more sympathy for the people who fumbled when they talked to us all those years ago about our gay identities.

Because we've learned from our mistakes and seen others do the same, we've become confident the art of identity conversations can be taught and learned just like any other skill. We now hope to impart that skill to you. What follows is a distillation of our years of work on how to say the right thing.

## Identity Conversations Are Difficult

Conversations about identity, diversity, and justice are some of the thorniest human interactions of our time. Consider these four real-life conversations:

> *A white male leader hosts a forum at his company about how non-Black employees can support their Black colleagues. In his opening remarks, he says he can relate to what Black people endure because he grew up Jewish in New York City and kids taunted him at school. He believes he's displaying empathy. His employees think he's out of touch.*

> *A woman is grocery shopping with her toddler son when they come across a baby girl with a medical condition that makes her skin red and scaly. The toddler yells: "Why is that baby so red?!" Mortified, the woman shushes her son and frog-marches him to the next aisle. The baby's father feels hurt. He wishes the woman had acknowledged his baby's condition openly and calmly.*

> *A millennial woman asks her boomer uncle at a family gathering to stop commenting on her friend's physical*

*attractiveness. He offers a barrage of defenses: "They were compliments," "Other women like the attention," and "I have a wife and daughters; I'm not a sexist." The woman leaves the conversation disheartened. The man leaves exasperated that younger generations take offense at everything.*

*A man accidentally uses the pronoun "he" instead of "she" to refer to a classmate who is a trans woman. He apologizes profusely, saying he still grapples with the privilege of being cisgender (having his gender identity match the sex assigned at birth). He repeatedly insists he's "the worst." The classmate finds the apology excessive. She wishes he'd said "sorry" once and moved on.*

Such conversations have long created discomfort for individuals from nondominant groups, including women, people of color, LGBTQ+ people, and disabled people. They get frustrated that people on the dominant side of identity conversations—men, white people, straight people, cisgender people, nondisabled people—don't know enough about the issues, don't bother to educate themselves, get defensive when challenged, or opt out of conversations altogether. Nonetheless, nondominant group members often keep their concerns to themselves. "I've been having conversations about race for decades," a Black woman colleague told us. "In every single one, my priority has been keeping white people comfortable: How will they react? Will they get offended? Will they retaliate against me?"

What's new about the present moment is that, as social psychologist Jennifer Richeson points out, discomfort is being "democratized"—the burden previously placed on one side of the conversation is now shifting to both. In times past, the consequences of making a mistake in these conversations felt relatively mild to many in the dominant group, similar to the repercussions for a breach of etiquette. Now such individuals are in a new era. They wonder: *What if I hurt someone I care about? What if I get canceled?* Technological developments, including the rise of social media, have amplified these concerns. Private conversations can be recorded on cell phones. Text messages and emails can be forwarded far beyond their intended audiences. Fleeting thoughts, often stripped of nuance and context, can become part of a permanent record after they're tweeted and retweeted to millions of people. As speechwriter Jon Favreau notes, social media "forces everyone to become politicians," crafting careful statements about their beliefs that then get "picked apart" by observers.

We welcome the democratization of discomfort. It jolts people to wake up to the inequities in their communities and rise to challenge them. Yet we also see how it causes many to feel disoriented and retreat in fear. As a result, the people who participate in these discussions with the greatest confidence are those on the fringes. At one extreme, well-versed progressives revel in their virtue and virtuosity, crafting intricate mazes of language and manners. At the opposite extreme, right-wing provocateurs relish bulldozing those mazes, taking any blowback as a badge of honor.

The majority in the middle tread gingerly. Journalist Emily Yoffe mourns the freedom she's lost as a writer due to the "little voice" in the back of her head that now asks if she'll "get creamed on social media." Political scientist Yascha Mounk laments that a "good number" of his students "don't feel comfortable saying what they really think." The *New York Times* profiled a group of self-described liberals who "care deeply about social justice" but feel exhausted, as one put it, by the "constant need to be wary" of being labeled "racist or anti-trans." An eminent university president told us he scripts all speeches that touch on diversity (and only those speeches), because he worries he might otherwise ad-lib his way into a career-ending error. Conversations that could foster empathy instead provoke fear. Rather than supporting the people who are suffering most, would-be allies are consumed by their own anxiety.

## Identity Conversations Are Inescapable

In earlier decades, many groups lacked the numbers or the power to speak up, which meant many important conversations simply didn't happen. Thanks to changing demographics and the courageous activism of marginalized groups, we now appear to have reached a tipping point. In the United States, the numbers of non-Christian people, people of color, and LGBTQ+ people have all been steadily increasing. As social dynamics shift, many disempowered groups finally feel safer to open conversations that once were closed.

Identity conversations are also everywhere because they're championed, and initiated, by younger individuals. As a senior leader at an entertainment company put it to us: "Young people join as new hires, and they want forums to discuss the 'systemic racism' and 'white supremacy' in our workplace." This no-holds-barred approach often shocks his older employees: "Whoa—we're not *that* bad, are we?" The age-based divide isn't solely between the oldest generations and the youngest ones. Andy Dunn, an entrepreneur in his early forties, asked a young adult from Generation Z to flag offensive language in a draft of his book. She left over a thousand comments in the document in less than a day.

As these conversations become more frequent, members of nondominant groups are finding fresh words to challenge injus-

tice. They now have "nonbinary" and "neurodiverse" to understand their own identities, "tone policing" and "mansplaining" to
describe inappropriate conversational practices, and "misogynoir"
and "toxic masculinity" to call out harmful biases and behaviors.
Language matters. As Gloria Steinem once observed, until the
term "sexual harassment" named what had been considered business as usual, society could do little about the behavior. Experiences that led before only to a vague sense that "something is off"
can now be named, contested, and made right.

The upshot of these developments is that conversations about
identity, diversity, and justice occur across nearly all areas of life.
In the workplace, you're increasingly likely to receive training on
"privilege," "unconscious bias," or "inclusive leadership." In larger
organizations, you might have the opportunity to supplement
such training with seminars on women's advancement, task forces
on racial equity, or events that celebrate LGBTQ+ pride month, all
administered by a chief diversity officer and a team of specialists.

If you belong to a younger generation, you'll probably encounter these conversations well before you enter the workforce.
Universities have offered courses and extracurricular programs
relating to identity for a long time. These days, many high schools
and elementary schools have an array of antiracism, equity, and
belonging programs. Some daycare centers even teach diversity
and inclusion to preschoolers.

More generally, we can't remember the last day we made it
through our morning news feed without encountering a conversation about identity. Over the past few decades, issues like
Islamophobia, undocumented immigration, same-sex marriage,
campus free speech, Black Lives Matter, the #MeToo movement,
trans rights, anti-Asian hate crimes, cancel culture, and critical

race theory have become national and international controversies. The breakneck cycle of identity talk seems only to accelerate each year. Such accounts in the media shape what people talk about in ordinary social interactions. It's hard to feel like a functioning member of society without participating in at least some of these discussions.

All of this means that in a single month, you might field a call from a teacher who says your sixth-grader made a racist comment at school, puzzle over how to give constructive feedback to an underperforming employee without coming across as biased, stumble through an apology after you accidentally offend a lesbian friend, and argue with your cousin on Facebook after he makes a xenophobic post. Whether you're a passionate advocate for social justice or just someone who wants to be more considerate of others, there's never been a better time to put in the effort to get these conversations right.

## Conversational Guidance Is Often Inadequate

Unfortunately, it's hard to find effective guidance to help you improve. An article in the *Economist* suggests the twelve most terrifying words in the English language are "I'm from human resources and I'm here to organize a diversity workshop."

Sometimes diversity leaders go wrong by pandering to privileged listeners. As the former diversity director of Apple stated: "There can be twelve white, blue-eyed, blond men in a room and they're going to be diverse too because they're going to bring a different life experience and life perspective to the conversation." At other times, leaders stoke the fear that anything participants say or do could lead them to be labeled bigots. A training resource influential in some diversity and inclusion circles warns that "objectivity," "worship of the written word," and a "sense of urgency" are aspects of a noxious "white supremacy culture." Hovering over both the coddling and the scolding approaches is the uneasy sense that diversity training lacks rigor. To give but one instance from a sad trove, we think back to an executive retreat held in a New Age resort with crystals dangling from the birches. The organizer bumped our talk a few hours because the "equine experience" had run long. That experience required leaders to deliver a speech in front of a horse. The horse would respond by whinnying or shying or pawing the ground. Interpreting these reactions, a horse whisperer gave feedback on whether the executive was showing inclusive leadership. We suspended judgment, reminding ourselves that equine therapy is a well-regarded treatment for certain conditions. When the executives returned, though, they seemed glum. Asked how the session had gone, one said: "Pretty bad. When I was speaking, the horse took a shit. The facilitator said, 'Don't worry—it doesn't mean you're not an inclusive leader. Sometimes a horse just needs to shit.'"

A whinny is never just a whinny. But sometimes, horseshit is just horseshit.

### A Path Forward

We think we can help.

Our center is dedicated to research-backed approaches to diversity and inclusion. Importantly, however, we didn't build our strategies in the ivory tower—we developed and tested them with organizations that invited us to share our expertise. Together and separately, we've taught tens of thousands of individuals from all walks of life to have more meaningful and effective conversations across their differences. We've employed traditional methods of instruction, like lectures and workshops, as well as more innovative techniques, such as theater-based case studies crafted by Broadway director Schele Williams. Our approach is based on scholarship to ensure it's rigorous, and on our experience in the field to ensure it's practical.

We think we see diversity and inclusion issues from a distinctive viewpoint based on the communities we serve—call it the view from the bridge. On one side, we work with an overwhelmingly liberal group of students with activist values. On the other, we interact with senior leaders of corporations, professional services firms, governmental bodies, foundations, sports teams, and educational institutions struggling to do better. We also find ourselves in a bridging role because of our social identities. As a gay Asian American Gen X man and a gay white millennial man, we're grateful both sides talk to us. Many women, people of color, and LGBTQ+ people, among others, enlist us as allies. Many members of dominant groups candidly share their fear that the "pendulum has swung too far" against them.

Based on what we've seen and heard, we believe the greatest need is for individuals in higher power positions to improve how they engage in identity conversations. We define "identity" expansively to include all major demographic classifications, such as race, ethnicity, gender, sexual orientation, gender identity, disability, religion, socioeconomic status, and age. We also mean "conversation" in a broad sense—talking face-to-face as well as sending a text message, writing an email, or posting on social media.

Our intended audience is similarly wide-ranging. People in "higher power positions" aren't just those with greater authority inside an organization, such as a boss or a teacher. They're also all people of good will who enter conversations from the more advantaged side based on their social identity—for example, men in conversations about gender, white people in conversations about race, and nondisabled people in conversations about disability. Often we'll use the term "ally" or "allies" as a shorthand for such individuals. By definition, the ally has more power than the person on the other side. If allies can improve their skills, the effects will be transformative.

Our focus on people with more power isn't as limiting as it may seem. Since everyone has baskets of advantage and disadvantage, everyone is in the ally position at times, and everyone benefits from the allyship of others. A white woman can be an ally to a man of color on issues of race; he can be her ally on issues of gender. More generally, while we primarily direct our advice to allies, we believe this book will help all participants in identity conversations do better. We particularly hope it will help people from nondominant groups name conversational dynamics they've experienced, and describe the standard they expect from allies in their lives.

We've structured the book around seven principles. We start by teaching you to "Beware the Four Conversational Traps" (Principle 1): avoid, deflect, deny, and attack. To help you escape those four traps, we invite you to "Build Resilience" (Principle 2) so that you feel more emotionally grounded, and to "Cultivate Curiosity" (Principle 3) so that you approach these conversations with an open mind.

After absorbing these foundational principles, we explore two common and challenging types of conversations: disagreements and apologies. We teach you to "Disagree Respectfully" (Principle 4) when you have an enduring difference of opinion and to "Apologize Authentically" (Principle 5) when you need to make amends.

We believe you will cause less harm to your conversation

partners if you follow these five principles, but we urge you to go further. In the medical profession, ethicists distinguish between non-maleficence ("do no harm") and beneficence ("do good"). Allyship also takes these two forms of "doing no harm" and "doing good." Our final two principles are intended to help allies go out into the world and make positive change in their social circles, educational institutions, workplaces, and local communities. We urge you to "Apply the Platinum Rule" (Principle 6) by helping people affected by bias as they wish to be helped, and we encourage you to "Be Generous to the Source" (Principle 7) by supporting those who have engaged in noninclusive behavior so they can grow past their mistakes.

These principles can't guarantee positive outcomes in all conversations—the proper approach to any dialogue is always some shade of "it depends." Yet we're confident you'll see an immediate improvement in the quality of your conversations if you follow these seven guidelines.

## Our Promises

Before we send you off to get started, we make three commitments to you.

First, we'll be relentlessly practical. We want to offer strategies you can put into place as soon as you read them. While the seven principles build on each other, they can also stand alone. You can use them as you would a portable tool kit, by picking whichever conversational tool you need at the time. What's more, we've erred on the side of brevity—our hope is that you can read this book in a few sittings.

Second, we promise there will be no shaming in this book. As with all good coaches, we'll sometimes tell you things you don't want to hear. Yet we sharply distinguish between pushing you hard to do better and berating you. Both of us spent many years of our upbringing in insular religious, cultural, or activist communities that had strict moral codes and harshly judged those who fell short. We found that approach unconducive to growth. The people we most admire in our field are those who combine compassion and rigor—who have the softest of hearts and the hardest of heads. We strive to adopt that same spirit in this book, in our work, and in our lives.

Last, and most important, we hope to galvanize you. Although we want to help you overcome your fear of saying the wrong thing, we set our sights far higher than teaching you tricks to avoid getting canceled. We hope by the time you finish this book you'll welcome many identity conversations. Instead of avoiding them, you'll see them as vital engines of justice.

Ours is a pivotal moment in history. On one side, people from disempowered groups are increasingly challenging behavior they had to tolerate in the past, and allies are standing with them. White people are going to rallies for Black Lives Matter and Stop Asian Hate. Men are joining the Women's March. Straight people are hoisting rainbow flags outside their windows for Pride. On the other side, opponents of inclusion are mobilizing in large numbers to undo long-standing rights and entrench inequalities. Whether our societies advance toward an inclusive future or backslide toward an unjust past is up to all of us.

We suspect you're reading this book because you already want to contribute to a more inclusive society but may not know where to start. How, after all, do you "dismantle the patriarchy" or "eliminate institutional racism"? Our own answer is to begin not on some grand scale, but in our local spheres of influence—families, friendship circles, neighborhoods, social media platforms, educational institutions, and workplaces. It's to hear those who speak of the inequities in our world, and to raise our voices as allies in support of their quest for justice. It's to say the right thing, not in the sense of obeying rules of etiquette, but in the sense of speaking up for what's right.

We've seen again and again that silences can find words, that words can become conversations, and that conversations can change lives. You have to start somewhere. For us, that place is here.

# Principle 1:

## Beware the Four Conversational Traps

Imagine you're a white person who hosts an annual holiday party. One of your closest friends, Amir, consistently declines your invitations. The first few years, you chalked it up to scheduling issues. Now you worry something's wrong. After all, Amir seems eager to catch up one-on-one. Over dinner, you broach the topic. To your horror, he tells you he feels awkward at your parties because they're so racially homogeneous. "It brings home to me that I'm one of your only friends of color," he says. "I just don't fit in there."

If you're like the people we work with, you may have one of four defensive reactions to Amir's comment:

- You *avoid* by falling silent or by remembering a phone call you have to make.

- You *deflect* by saying you didn't intend to exclude anyone or by changing the topic of conversation to the latest episode of your favorite TV series.

- You *deny* by invoking the non-white friends who have attended in the past or by doubting whether Amir really feels awkward given his apparent comfort in other all-white settings.

- You *attack* by asking Amir why he makes everything about race or by suggesting he's a hypocrite for hosting parties that lack diversity himself.

Don't despair if this catalog feels familiar. You're not alone. Some experts on conversations about race wonder if white people are "reciting lines from a shared script" or if they "all learn the lines from the same sheet" given how uniform their responses are. We think such scripts appear in all kinds of identity conversations, and white people aren't the only ones reading from them. These behaviors are normal human responses to feeling defensive. We ourselves lapse into them all the time.

On the bright side, these patterns make it easy to spot the unhelpful reactions, which makes them easier to change. When we coach people, we use the acronym A.D.D.A. to help them remember the four conversational traps of avoid, deflect, deny, and attack. If you learn to reduce your reliance on A.D.D.A., you'll already be well on your way to having better conversations.

## Avoid

Former Fox News host Eric Bolling walked off a live interview on the BBC show *Newsnight* not once, but twice. Major League Baseball had just relocated the 2021 All-Star Game from Atlanta to Denver to protest a Georgia voting law that disproportionately denied Black voters

access to the vote. Bolling argued this decision would hurt its sup-
posed beneficiaries by harming Black-owned businesses in Georgia.

His conversation partner, political strategist Aisha Moodie-Mills,
was having none of it. "I think it's really rich for any Republican,
especially a white man, to run around and claim that they care about
the economic condition of Black communities," she said. "I'm done,"
Bolling bellowed as he rose from his seat and stalked out of the shot.
At the request of the host, Emily Maitlis, he returned a few moments
later and repeatedly demanded an apology. When Moodie-Mills
refused, Bolling disengaged. "I'm done," he repeated, before depart-
ing again, this time for good.

Bolling demonstrated the most common negative response:
avoidance. People dodge all manner of conversations about identity. A nondisabled man told diversity consultant Diane Goodman
he avoids disabled people altogether because he can't figure out
how "to walk the line between acknowledging a difference in ability and being rude; between helpfulness and patronization." A senior leader confided in us that he'd unearthed the perfect solution
to manage generational differences: "I don't understand millenni-
als. I don't know how to talk to them. So I avoid them entirely." At a
recent family gathering, one of our students got into a living-room
discussion about trans rights with her relatives. "Within seconds,"
she said, "half the guests fled to talk in the kitchen instead."

Sometimes you might leave the room because you refuse to
dignify an off-putting comment with a response. Bolling might
cast his walkout in these terms, given that Moodie-Mills accused
him of being hypocritical partly because he's a white man. In
identity conversations, however, you'll constantly encounter comments you consider unfair. If you withdraw every time, you'll shut
down all engagement, leaving your conversation partner to feel
even more frustrated and unheard.

Another avoidance strategy is to go silent. A global pharmaceutical company once asked us to run a diversity workshop for its leaders that included time for small-group discussion. On a planning call, the internal lead asked us what to do if participants stared at each other silently the entire time. We observed that these leaders were high-ranking employees who—to put it delicately—weren't the type to withhold their opinions. "Yes," she sighed, "they're talkative on every subject but this one."

Silence may seem relatively safe. But members of nondominant groups are increasingly, and rightly, calling it out as an abdication of responsibility. Writer Savala Nolan argues that people of color "hear" and "feel" the silence of white peers, understanding it to mean: "I don't have your back. Or I don't care enough to get uncomfortable to speak out." During recent spikes in antisemitism, including a spate of vandalized synagogues and a rise in pro-Nazi hate speech, many Jewish people expressed frustration at those who were outspoken on other issues of social justice but ignored this one. "I am saddened and appalled by the lack of outreach . . . and overwhelming silence when it comes to the struggles of my people," lamented activist Alexandra Tsuneta.

Members of dominant groups are starting to realize that such silence is untenable. Writing in 2020, organizational scholars Robin Ely and David Thomas described how a white senior partner in a global professional services firm was at a total loss for words during the Black Lives Matter protests. But he steeled himself to find them. He recognized that "if he said nothing about the recent racist incidents, his silence would speak for him, with a message not of neutrality but of complicity."

The final, most subtle form of avoidance is to not say what you really think. In conversations about identity, this approach often means saying something "nice" rather than something true.

We think of a Facebook meme of a smiling child standing in her living room with one natural leg and one prosthetic leg made of metal. The tagline reads: "I didn't see a disability. I only saw the beauty of her smile!" We understand why allies share this meme. People from majority groups often think it's kindest to emphasize commonalities and ignore differences. They believe this approach sends the message that kids with disabilities are just as beautiful as kids without them. Yet many in the disability community hear a different message. To them, such comments suggest disability is something shameful that decent people overlook. As disability activist Carly Findlay puts it: "When you say 'I don't see your disability,' you invalidate who I am." It's the same suggestion that leads many gay people to feel hurt if you say "I don't think of you as gay" or many people of color to feel invalidated if you say "I don't see color." Members of these groups certainly don't want you to see them as *only* disabled, gay, or non-white, but pretending you can't see their identity at all is an overcorrection.

This form of avoidance can also involve expressing your real views but fobbing them off onto others, such as by saying, "I think *other people* might argue . . . ," "My friend, who is far more old-fashioned than I am, might say . . . ," or by claiming to take a position solely for the sake of argument. According to writer Melissa Fabello, when a feminist posts an article about the gender wage gap on the internet, men will tell her "that the statistics are faulty, that women take more time off of work, that women just don't like STEM fields—all under the guise of 'playing devil's advocate.'" Instead of presenting fake views as your own, this move presents your actual views as someone else's. In both cases, your conversation partner will often sense you're just not owning your opinions.

By criticizing "avoid" behavior, we're not suggesting you need to dive headlong into every identity conversation and stay engaged no matter what. Not all behavior that looks like avoidance is. Sometimes you need to process what you've heard, learn more about the subject, or think about what to say before you blurt out something you regret. We call this more benign form of disengagement "taking an off-ramp"—pausing the conversation to get in the right frame of mind before you re-enter it later. The key distinction is that one behavior is reflexive and the other is reflective. Hiding in the corner because you don't want to engage at all is avoidance. Temporarily stepping out of a conversation so you can bring your best self to the dialogue is not.

## Deflect

When you deflect, you don't literally or figuratively leave the conversation. You instead shift attention from the topic under discussion to a more comfortable topic of your choosing.

### DEFLECTING TO TONE

One of our students, Victoria, served on the board of an LGBTQ+ nonprofit that included alumni of her college. Some alums admonished the predominantly white organization on its Facebook group for ignoring the concerns of LGBTQ+ people of color. The board responded with new community engagement guidelines that threatened to expel members from the Facebook group if they didn't frame their criticisms more courteously. Victoria denounced these guidelines. She observed that white people had made unkind comments in the past without the board calling for better manners, and that this new policy seemed to value "tone policing over antiracism." Board members came down on her for being rude and disrespectful. "Have you no decency?" one asked.

Tone policing occurs when you deflect attention from *what*

your conversation partner says to *how* they said it. It's a familiar frustration shared by many members of nondominant groups. Writer Layla Saad says tone policing asks people of color to talk about racism "without sharing any of our (real) emotions about it." Ironically, in Victoria's case, she was tone policed for objecting to tone policing.

A disability advocate, Daniela, described a subtler form of tone policing at her university. During the COVID-19 pandemic, she found the university's shift to remote learning bittersweet. On the one hand, she admired how seamlessly the administration pivoted from in-person to virtual classes. On the other, she was heartbroken over how swiftly it adopted policies like captioning and recording lectures that disability advocates at the school had sought for years. Previously, the administration had told her such changes were impossible.

Daniela went to the president of the university for assurance the school would be more open to accommodations for disabilities in the future. Early in the conversation, she made the blunder of saying it pained her to see how "easy" the transition to remote learning had been. The president took offense at Daniela's use of the word "easy" and fastened on it for the rest of the conversation, lecturing her on how implementing these reforms had been a massive and exhausting effort. Rather than focusing on the substance of Daniela's point, he fixated on the way she expressed it.

To be sure, tone matters. Yet especially when worked up about injustice, even the calmest person can raise their voice or choose an overheated adjective. As the individual on the receiving end, you may feel genuinely wounded by your conversation partner's tone. We know we sometimes do. But chiding someone for not being flawlessly composed turns a conversation that should be about the other person's concerns into a conversation about your feelings.

## DEFLECTING BY CHANNEL SWITCHING

In a horrific shooting spree, a man opened fire in three Atlanta-area massage businesses. He killed eight individuals, including six women of Asian descent. Media coverage focused on the racial dimensions of the shooting. It compared the anti-Asian hatred to the anti-Black hatred the Black Lives Matter movement had brought into the national conversation. After the shooting, an online civil rights forum teemed with activity. One white woman, Nancy, wrote a post on the forum criticizing the media for ignoring the gender angle, noting the victims were almost all women. One colleague responded to Nancy's post, thanking her for raising issues of "intersectionality." A term coined by legal scholar Kimberlé Crenshaw, intersectionality refers to the distinctive experiences of individuals who belong to more than one marginalized group—in this case, "Asian" and "woman."

As it turned out, Nancy didn't want to expand the frame from "race" to "race and gender." Instead, she wanted to change the topic from "only race" to "only gender." She argued the shooter showed hostility to women, not hostility to Asians. Other colleagues gently, then not so gently, pointed out how she'd flipped the media's simplistic view that "this is about race, not gender" into a similarly simplistic view that "this is about gender, not race." The shootings, they claimed, could be—and were—about both.

Nancy doubled down. She defended her stance by saying that throughout history, women only made political gains—like securing the right to vote—when they refused to focus on "any other form of oppression except sex." Women of color in the conversation, as well as their allies, blasted this position. Shortly after, the moderator shut down the conversation and asked all participants to take the debate offline.

Nancy's insistence on shifting focus from one group to another is an example of "channel switching." In fairness, the channel should be switched if the original programming is off base. But people often change the channel only to shift attention from a topic they find uncomfortable. In an episode of the *Journal of the American Medical Association* podcast titled "Structural Racism for Doctors—What Is It?," physician Mitch Katz offered examples of racial disparities in housing, education, and healthcare. The interviewer, Ed Livingston, volleyed back that the issue "isn't racism" but a "socioeconomic phenomenon." Of course, Livingston is entitled to that opinion. Yet given that he was hosting a talk on "structural racism," Livingston showed a puzzling resistance to the topic. His own discomfort seemed to be playing a critical role: "Personally I think taking racism out of the conversation would help. Many people like myself are offended by the implication that we are somehow racist."

In addition to switching "across" groups, channel switching can also occur "up" or "down." "Upswitching" occurs when someone responds to the slogan "Black Lives Matter" by saying "All Lives Matter." That person isn't shunting the discussion across to another group, but up to our universal humanity. A doctor friend of ours encountered upswitching when he organized an event for employees at his hospital to talk about the Black Lives Matter movement. A white woman approached him afterward to say the event should have discussed all marginalized groups, including women, LGBTQ+ people, and people with disabilities.

"Downswitching" is the opposite move—switching from a broad topic to a narrow one. A white male colleague once told us he disliked conversations about "privilege" because the term encompassed too much. He felt that identity conversations should concentrate on the topic of race, and in particular on Black individuals.

In all forms of channel switching—across, up, and down—the

result is to divert attention from whatever issue your conversation partner has raised. Nondominant groups find it hard enough to get airtime as it is. Staying on topic is the least you can do. If you believe another channel is receiving inadequate attention, the better strategy is not to switch away from the other person's channel, but to raise your own channel as a separate topic (perhaps at a later time). Had Nancy opened a discussion about sexism without shutting down people who were desperate to be heard on the topic of race, a more productive conversation might have ensued.

## DEFLECTING TO YOURSELF

In a law course some years ago, a student approached the professor after class. During his lecture, the professor had repeatedly used the phrase "illegal alien." The student asked him to reconsider using the term. The professor defended himself by saying the assigned cases used it. The student responded that the cases were old and the term was now widely considered dehumanizing. She suggested he use "undocumented immigrant" instead.

At that moment, the professor said it stung to be criticized on these points, as he had a distinguished record of advocating for civil rights. The student said the professor's record was why she felt comfortable raising this issue. It became clear, however, that the professor couldn't get beyond the perceived assault on his reputation. The student gave up and left the room.

In this form of deflection, you divert attention from an accusation of wrongdoing by appealing to your character as a good person. It's one of many categories of deflecting to yourself. The most dreaded form of this deflection—"Some of my best friends are Black"—is now roundly ridiculed. Yet many kindred phrases are still in wide circulation, such as "I grew up in a diverse neighborhood" or "I'm in an interracial marriage."

Another form of deflection to yourself is to point not to how good you are, but to how bad you've had it. In an ingenious study, researchers L. Taylor Phillips and Brian Lowery conducted a set of experiments to test how white respondents reacted when confronted with their privilege. The researchers asked one group to describe their childhood. They asked the other group to describe their childhood as well, but only after reading a prompt that included these lines: "White Americans enjoy many privileges that Black Americans do not. White Americans are advantaged in the domains of academics, housing, healthcare, jobs, and more compared to Black Americans." The group that read the prompt described having worse childhoods than the group that didn't.

Obviously, the two randomly divided groups didn't have such different childhoods. The researchers inferred that participants felt threatened by the reminder of their advantages. Those who didn't read the prompt were able to describe their childhoods freely. Those who read the prompt, however, needed to claim hardship to feel better about themselves. This "hard-knock life effect" has also been replicated in the context of socioeconomic status, where students from elite universities responded with their own adversities when reminded of their class privilege.

Occasionally the impulse behind this form of deflection is self-absorbed: "I don't need to think about your hardship, because I'm suffering too." But it can also come from an attempt gone wrong to build commonalities. In one conversation, a Latina colleague of ours, Xiomara, described sadly how she called herself an Anglicized nickname she hated, "Zara," because non-Hispanic people couldn't be bothered to learn how to pronounce her real name. Susan, a white woman, responded: "I know how you feel. A lot of people call me Suzy and I hate it." Everyone but Susan immediately cringed. We saw what Susan was trying to do—make Xiomara feel less alone. Yet having a common, easily pronounced name shortened to a nickname is not the same as being forced to hide one's cultural identity to assimilate. Susan could have expressed empathy for Xiomara without trying to build a bridge too far.

Then there's the "good intentions" defense. In response to Donald Trump's stance on immigration, television personality Kelly Osbourne asked in a live appearance on *The View*: "If you kick every Latino out of this country, then who is going to be cleaning your toilet, Donald Trump?" Actor Rosie Perez, who was also on the panel, pushed back: "Latinos are not the only people doing that." Osbourne jumped to her intentions: "I didn't mean it like that. Come on. No, I would never mean it like that."

Of course, a person's intentions do matter. Many distinctions in the law—say, between murder and manslaughter—turn on intent. Yet such blanket statements—"I didn't mean it like that," "I meant well," "My intentions were good"—distract from the harm. Just as it's possible to physically injure someone by accident, it's possible to invoke harmful stereotypes by accident as well.

## Deny

Do women get interrupted more than men? We thought the answer was obvious to everyone until we discussed it with a group of fifty lawyers, most of whom were men. We were running a training session in a marbled room with floor-to-ceiling views of the city skyline. To meet the participants where they lived, we used research that looked at how often justices on the United States Supreme Court were interrupted during oral arguments. According to the study, women justices—who made up only 22 percent of the court over the span studied—fielded 54 percent of all interruptions.

We started the discussion by asking whether anyone in the room had observed women being interrupted more than men. Amazingly, the first three people to jump in with their observations were men. Each proclaimed he'd seen no such behavior. "This is a high-octane, intense environment," one insisted. "Everyone gets interrupted. We're equal-opportunity offenders." They didn't fight the research, but argued that, somehow, their law firm was exempt from the dynamic it identified.

Eventually a woman began to speak. Another man deliberately interrupted her, making a joke about how women get interrupted. By then, two of the women had tears in their eyes and others were grimacing. We realized we had a lot more work to do with this organization.

The men in this firm fell into the third conversational trap: denial. Denial takes conversations about identity into openly hostile territory. When you deny, you're finally addressing the identity issue in question. Unfortunately, you're doing so just to dismiss what the other person is saying.

Deniers often announce from their objective perch that their conversation partner is categorically wrong, no questions asked. In a notable example, journalist Megyn Kelly dismissed calls for more racially diverse representations of Santa Claus by insisting: "Santa just *is* white. . . . Santa is what he is." This comment was strange mostly because Santa is a fictional character. It was also strange because even the historical figure of Saint Nicholas hailed from what is now called Turkey and likely didn't resemble contemporary depictions of Santa at all.

The other major kind of denial relates to feelings rather than facts. In its most gobsmacking form, someone denies that another person's emotions are real. When Comedy Central anointed Trevor Noah as Jon Stewart's successor to host *The Daily Show*, critics pointed to old tweets of Noah's they alleged were antisemitic and sexist. In one tweet, Noah joked that "behind every successful rap billionaire is a double as rich Jewish man." In others, he compared women's hockey to "lesbian porn" and mocked "fat chicks." Rising to Noah's defense, fellow comedian Jim Norton proclaimed Noah's critics were faking their reactions: "Their outrage is a lie and their motives are transparent. They are simply using his tweets to get their dopamine drip." (Noah appeared to take a different view, noting the jokes didn't reflect his "evolution as a comedian.") Matt Groening, creator of *The Simpsons*, had a similar comeback to Norton's. Critics had suggested the show's South Asian character, Apu, was insulting, in part because he managed a convenience store, fathered eight children through an arranged marriage, and had a heavy Indian accent voiced by a white actor. South Asian American comedian Hari Kondabolu noted he was bullied as a child because of the Apu character. Groening was nonchalant: "I think it's a time in our culture where people love to pretend they're offended."

More regularly, deniers acknowledge that the other person's feeling is real but claim it's illegitimate. They might accuse their conversation partner of being "oversensitive," "thin-skinned," "humorless," or a "snowflake." When comedian and actor Kevin Hart landed the coveted job of hosting the Academy Awards, it reignited a controversy about Hart's history of making antigay comments. Among other remarks, Hart had called one person on Twitter a "fat fag" and another a "gay billboard for AIDS," and had said having a gay son was one of his "biggest fears." When asked for an explanation years later, he said he'd no longer make such comments because times are more "sensitive" now in that "we love to make big deals out of things that aren't necessarily big deals." Hart's refusal to offer a proper apology led the Academy to ask him to step down as host.

We think Hart was right to observe that times are more sensitive now. We just don't think of that sensitivity in negative terms. If you watch a decades-old TV show or movie today, we think you'll be stunned by the blatant racism, sexism, homophobia, and transphobia, even in shows styled as family entertainment. It's fine to think society has overcorrected for those harms and become sensitive to a fault. But we encourage you to express those disagreements thoughtfully, which we discuss in Principle 4 (Disagree Respectfully). Unlike respectful disagreement, denial is again reflexive, not reflective. The denier rejects the other person's perspective out of hand, without any openness to the possibility of being wrong.

## Attack

After years of research and production, pop musician Sia announced the "news you've been waiting for!" on Twitter. The tweet linked to a preview of her directorial debut film, *Music*, which portrayed a teenage girl with autism.

To her surprise, Sia received scalding criticism from disability advocates, who were appalled that she cast a non-autistic actor in the central role. "Creating work on disability without disabled input is ableist and dismissive," said one. "It's a mighty shame that someone with such a colossal platform is using it to exclude disabled and neurodiverse actors from their own narratives," said another.

It's understandable that after years of toil, a film director would feel defensive when taking criticism from individuals who hadn't seen the work. Yet Sia went ballistic. One autistic actor said she could have played the role and that "zero effort was made" to include autistic people. Sia replied, "Fucking bullshit. You have no fucking idea because you weren't there and haven't seen the movie," adding, "maybe you're just a bad actor." When asked if she did any research or consulted the autistic community in casting the role, Sia responded: "Duh. I spent three fucking years researching." As she left the conversation, her parting words aptly summarized her feelings: "Fuckity fuck why don't you watch my film before you judge it? FURY."

Sia's outburst represents the last and most aggressive behavior in an identity conversation—an attack. This behavior is like denial in that you engage with the issue and push back on what you're hearing. But it differs in being more combative and more personal.

Writer Ijeoma Oluo endured an even more egregious outburst than Sia's when she challenged a white Canadian man who told her on Twitter that racism doesn't exist in Canada. Initially, the man was friendly, inviting her to come to his country to escape the racism in the United States. Because this was Twitter, several Canucks of color jumped in to supply examples of Canadian racism. Nevertheless, the man persisted in his original view. When Oluo pointed out "the irony of stating that racism doesn't exist, while talking over, belittling, and denying the lived experiences of Canadians of color," he responded by accusing her of calling him racist and by hurling a vulgar slur at her in all-caps. To make matters worse, he then cyberstalked and harassed her.

Online spaces are notoriously vicious, but such bad behavior isn't limited to the internet. Actor Laurence Fox went into attack mode in a discussion regarding Prince Harry and Duchess of Sussex Meghan Markle on a BBC current affairs program. Markle had been subjected to fevered tabloid coverage in Great Britain from the moment she and Prince Harry became engaged. A biracial woman, Markle received blistering criticism for her relationship history, her clothing choices, the food she ate, and even the way she crossed her legs while seated. Many analysts saw racialized double standards in how Markle was covered relative to Prince William's wife, Kate Middleton.

Commenting on Markle and Prince Harry's announcement that they were stepping back from the royal family, Fox argued they were trying to have it both ways by leaving the family while retaining some benefits of royal status. Rachel Boyle, a Black woman in the audience who happened to be a scholar of race, responded: "The problem we've got with this is that Meghan has agreed to be Harry's wife, and then the press have torn her to pieces. And let's be really clear about what this is. Let's call it by its name. It's racism."

Fox started by denying the coverage was racist: "It's not racism. You can't just—it's not racism." Boyle responded: "It absolutely is." Fox was insistent, and now angry: "It's not. We're the most tolerant, lovely country in Europe. . . . It's so easy to throw the charge of racism at everybody, and it's really starting to get boring."

The conversation took a fateful turn when Boyle gently suggested Fox might lack relevant knowledge: "What worries me about your comment is: you are a white privileged male who has no experience in this." As soon as Boyle uttered the words "white privileged male," the mostly white audience let out a collective groan. As if drawing energy from that response, Fox went nuclear. "Oh, *God*," he grunted while rolling his eyes and lowering his head to the table. "I can't help what I am. I was born like this. It's an immutable characteristic. So to call me a 'white privileged male' is to be racist. You're being racist."

We suspect you've got enough self-control not to behave like Sia, the man Oluo describes as "Mr. Friendly Canadian," or Fox. Yet attacks can also be subtler, such as passive-aggressive behavior or sarcasm. Most of us at times engage in these more understated forms of attack.

꙳

We want to complete our whistle-stop tour of avoid, deflect, deny, and attack (A.D.D.A.) by acknowledging that these behaviors don't always come from a bad place. The actions themselves are usually unconscious and all too human in origin. Identity conversations feel threatening—they challenge bedrock beliefs and frequently seem to call your integrity into question. It's only natural you jump into fight-or-flight mode by walking out of the room, changing the subject, resisting what the other person is telling you, or bringing the war into their camp. Even as diversity and inclusion scholars, we struggle to overcome these ingrained behaviors.

To be an ally, however, requires you to make an effort to move from a reflexive response to a reflective one. Think of how frustrating it would be to attempt to speak with someone about an experience of bias or an issue of justice that's critical to your sense of self, only for the other person to focus more on managing their own discomfort through A.D.D.A. That frustration would intensify if, rather than just encountering this behavior once, you encountered it again and again.

The move from reflexive to reflective can be immensely difficult when your conversation partner's behavior seems unfair. Maybe they dismissed your hard work like Sia's Twitter critics dismissed hers. Maybe their tone sounded disrespectful or they came across as oversensitive, because you didn't *mean* harm. Maybe they were just plain wrong. Even so, in all these situations, we challenge you to rise to your highest aspirations rather than running away or justifying yourself right out of the gate. The other person may be behaving less than optimally because they've been hurt or misunderstood in the past. It's now up to you to continue the cycle or break it. Remember why you enter these dialogues in the first place: to support people who need allies.

When you take a beat to reflect instead of launching into A.D.D.A. behavior, you might still end up with the same viewpoint or even use the same words. But it will come from a more considered and more respectful place. To get there, you'll have to control the surge of emotion that leads you to react rather than engage. As you will see, the most foundational skill you need to develop is resilience.

## Principle 1 **TAKEAWAYS**

- To improve at identity conversations, start by guarding against four conversational traps: avoid, deflect, deny, and attack (A.D.D.A.).

- *Avoid* refers to physically leaving the conversation, remaining silent, or not saying what you really think.

- *Deflect* refers to changing the subject, such as to the other person's tone, to another disempowered group, or to your own progressive credentials, hardships, or good intentions.

- *Deny* refers to reflexively dismissing whatever the other person says, such as by rejecting facts, the sincerity of their feelings, or the legitimacy of those feelings.

- *Attack* refers to combative, personal affronts, such as insults, sarcasm, eye-rolling, and passive-aggressive behavior.

# Principle 2:

# Build Resilience

It was a typical meeting at the school that Kenji's children attend. A couple dozen earnest parents were crowded around cafeteria tables pushed together to make an open square big enough to seat them all. The group was digesting the results of a recent survey relating to anti-Black racism at the school and peer institutions. The accounts were searing—students described how classmates had called them the n-word and told them they were admitted only because of affirmative action. Kenji was shocked at these findings and characterized the moment as an existential crisis. He then wondered aloud why so few of the Black parents in the group were speaking out about it.

He got his answer quickly. Alicia, a Black woman, didn't raise her voice, but filled it with authority: "I think this is a check-your-privilege moment, Kenji. This may be news to you because your children don't get called the n-word. Mine do. I don't speak up because I live this every day." Other parents shuffled uncomfortably in their seats and waited for Kenji to respond.

Given Kenji's role as the faculty director of a center devoted to diversity and inclusion, you might assume that he responded with openness and grace. Sadly, you'd be wrong. His primary reaction was a rage that surprised even him. His internal monologue went something like: *How dare you tell me to check my privilege! I grew up gay at a time when same-sex relationships were criminalized. I was routinely told I'd never have kids, so the fact I have kids at all, much less at this school, is the miraculous result of a lifelong struggle. You should check your privilege!* Though he kept these thoughts to himself, he withdrew from the discussion.

David experienced a similar emotional upheaval. He was on a virtual call with several senior professionals of color in the entertainment industry who had spent years advocating for their field to become more diverse and inclusive. David was helping them prep for a critical meeting with a group of mostly white producers. As they were trying to figure out what tone to strike during the upcoming meeting, David told them: "The producers are happy to engage with you because you're nice." Some people in the room looked down or furrowed their brows. Then one woman in the room, Pamela, called him out: "David, we're respected in our industry because of our hard work and accomplishments, not because we're 'nice.'"

Again, you might expect a researcher of diversity and inclusion to take such criticism in his stride. Yet David's immediate reaction was self-pity. He thought: *That's not what I meant! She's misinterpreting me!* The self-pity quickly morphed into guilt. As the youngest and only white person in the meeting, he'd somehow managed to congratulate a room full of senior people of color—many of whom had won their industry's most coveted laurels—on their nice tone. *What must they think of me?* he wondered. *Probably that I'm condescending and dismissive, perhaps even a racist—just another*

*white guy who pretends to be an ally but ends up disappointing the
people he's trying to support.*

꙰

Conversations about identity, diversity, and justice trigger acute
emotional reactions. If you've ever been told to check your privilege or accused of bias, you know what we mean. Yet even ordinary chitchat can provoke intense discomfort. When journalist
Joanne Lipman was sitting next to a businessman on a flight, she
mentioned she was about to speak at a women's conference. Her
previously friendly seatmate froze: "Sorry! Sorry I'm a man." He
explained that he had recently attended a diversity training where
the facilitator had "beaten up" the men in the room. It had felt like
"being sent to the principal's office" or "being sat in the corner."
He and Lipman spent the rest of the flight in a stiff silence.

What's going on here? Why would an adult come unglued at
the mere mention of a women's conference? Our best guess is that
he heard it as a personal attack. Whether the topic is bias in the
classroom, poverty in Indigenous communities, or the #MeToo
movement, all identity conversations suggest that some people
(like Lipman) experience unfair hardship because of a particular
social identity while others (like her seatmate) don't. These conversations can sound like you're being accused of blithely benefit-
ing from or ignoring another group's suffering.

As excruciating as it can feel to have conversations about
identity, it's important to remember people from nondominant
groups have always experienced emotional turmoil in these dialogues from being ignored, mocked, tone policed, or subjected
to retaliation. When you find yourself wondering, "Why am I so
uncomfortable?" you might instead ask, "Why have I been comfortable until now?" You might then hear the answer: "I've been

comfortable because until today, the other person has carried all the discomfort on their own."

The most immediate response you can make when you're feeling acutely uncomfortable is to take an off-ramp—the temporary break from a conversation we described in Principle 1 (Beware the Four Conversational Traps). Off-ramps will help you ward off the worst outcomes in these conversations, but they're usually not enough on their own to keep you emotionally grounded for the long haul. If you don't adopt more concrete strategies to build emotional resilience, you'll risk backsliding into "avoid," "deflect," "deny," or "attack" behavior at the first sign of distress.

## Adopt a Growth Mindset

The children's book *The Magical Yet* addresses a child who can't get the hang of riding a bike and gives up trying. In the book's illustrations, the child walks along a bike path sulking until she happens upon a glowing pink orb in the bushes known as The Magical Yet. With the Yet's help, the child learns to persist whenever she makes a mistake, whether it involves playing a musical instrument, learning a language, or riding a skateboard. "No matter how big (or old) you may get," the book observes, "you'll never outgrow—you'll never forget—you can always believe in the magic of Yet."

*The Magical Yet* tracks psychologist Carol Dweck's celebrated argument that people should move from a "fixed mindset" to a "growth mindset." Individuals with a fixed mindset believe their basic qualities—their intelligence, personality, talents, and moral character—are basically unchangeable. If they're not good at something, they probably never will be and should give up trying. Individuals with a growth mindset, in contrast, believe they can cultivate their qualities through effort. Across a variety of fields, from relationships to sports to business leadership, Dweck shows that a growth mindset leads to greater success. It prevents people from treating every setback as a verdict on their innate competence and moral worth.

This simple and crucial concept has taken over institutions from corporations to preschools, helping people recover from mistakes and improve their skills. Yet as our NYU colleague and social psychologist Dolly Chugh points out, the concept is glaringly absent from discussions of identity. She explains that people get mired in a fixed mindset on identity issues because the costs of making a mistake seem catastrophic. If you make a mistake when learning a musical instrument, you probably won't be traumatized. Yet if you make a mistake on an identity issue, you haven't just made an error—you've become a racist, a sexist, or a homophobe. Something you *did* comes to describe who you *are*. The perceived threat is so huge it's no wonder you're panicked. But that terror means you won't even try to learn. Imagine if we began a class by saying: "Our one requirement for the semester is that you not make any mistakes."

As Chugh argues, you won't make progress until you let go of the fixed-mindset outlook that you're either a good or bad person and embrace the growth-mindset idea that you're a "good-ish" person. If you insist you're a good person, you're likely to react with overwhelming discomfort when you make a mistake that would reveal your imperfections. If, by contrast, you acknowledge you're a "good-ish" person who falters like everybody else, you're less likely to see mistakes as judgments of your character. You can then respond by treating mistakes as opportunities to learn.

Social science research backs up the idea that a fixed mindset derails identity conversations. In a series of experiments,

Dweck and her colleagues found that participants with the fixed-mindset view that prejudice is unchangeable were less interested in having cross-racial interactions or learning about bias than people who believed prejudice can change through effort. In one experiment, white participants were put in a room and told they were about to speak with either a Black or white partner. When they expected a Black partner, those with a fixed mindset tended to place their seats farther away from the other person and expressed a desire for shorter interactions than those with a growth mindset. In another experiment, white participants with a fixed mindset made less eye contact, smiled less, and had a faster heart rate in cross-racial interactions. These findings held true even when controlling for the participants' racial attitudes.

A fixed mindset might also trip you up in a sneakier way. In a separate study, Dweck and her colleague gave college students who did poorly on a test the opportunity to look at the completed tests of other students. Students with a fixed mindset tended to look at the tests of students who performed worse than they did. They didn't think they could do better, so they settled for easing their discomfort. Students with a growth mindset tended to look at the tests of students who performed better than they did. Because they knew they could improve, they eagerly explored how to do so. A telltale sign of a fixed mindset in identity conversations is the urge to compare yourself to people more biased or gaffe-prone than you. In a growth mindset, you compare yourself to people who display the most inclusive behavior, not the least. Next time you're at a family dinner and you mess up, watch out for those downward comparisons: "At least I'm not as bad as Aunt Edith!" Try to inspire yourself with role models instead: "What would Aunt Nell say to make this right?"

When you slip into a fixed mindset, we recommend two techniques. The first is to summon The Magical Yet from the bushes and add the word "yet" to the end of negative self-talk. It's not: "I'm not good at talking about race." It's: "I'm not good at talking about race, yet." Educators use this technique a lot. Kenji's children are not allowed to utter the words "I'm not good at math" at school. Their teachers insist they say: "I'm not good at math, yet."

The second technique is to do a self-comparison. Instead of "My younger colleagues find it so much easier to talk about mental health than I do," you might say, "I find it easier to talk about mental health than I did a year ago." We realize this recommendation sits in tension with our other recommendation to engage in upward comparisons to others. But here—and in general—our strategies aren't mutually exclusive. Take whichever one works for you. If you find it inspiring to compare yourself to role models, do so. If you find it stressful or demoralizing, make self-comparisons instead. Regardless of the technique, the goal is to catch yourself when you're feeling fatalistic and substitute thinking that's both more honest and more compassionate.

When she visited our center, civil rights lawyer Chai Feldblum discussed her own struggles with this mindset shift. Feldblum is an iconic figure in American law and a principal author of the Americans with Disabilities Act. Despite her credentials, she told us during an event how she used to dread making mistakes in identity conversations. Whenever she made an error in the past, she said, "all I would do is berate myself." Yet over a period of years, she learned to focus on growing from the mistake instead of letting it define her.

Feldblum asked us to imagine saying something inadvertently hurtful to a person with a disability. "If you're not in the disability culture," she said, "I assure you, you may not know that something you said did not feel good to that person." She then shared her recommended form of self-talk in response to that mistake: "Wow, I guess I just wasn't ever taught that or thought about that." This shift—from "I'm a terrible human being" to "I just wasn't ever taught that"—offers you the gift of redemption. And importantly, as Feldblum noted, it grants you the opportunity to behave differently next time. If you didn't learn it before, you can learn it now.

## Self-Affirm

In a recurring segment on *Saturday Night Live* starting in the 1990s, the character of Stuart Smalley hosted a mock self-help show. "Stuart Smalley is a caring nurturer, a member of several twelve-step programs, but not a licensed therapist," the narrator would say. Smalley, a middle-aged man in a cardigan with perfectly coiffed bleached-blond hair, would then appear on-screen. Smalley started each episode by gazing at himself in the mirror, taking a deep breath, and solemnly intoning: "I'm going to do a terrific show today. And I'm going to help people. Because I'm good enough. I'm smart enough. And doggone it, people like me!"

Smalley's affirmations were so syrupy that they always made the audience laugh. Yet Smalley may be enjoying the last laugh these days. Ample social science backs up the gist of his approach. Self-affirmation has been used to help people absorb threatening health information, improve performance at school, and reduce prejudice against other social groups. Psychologists Geoffrey Cohen and David Sherman note that the technique allows people to take a "psychological time-out" and "see the many ordinary stressors of daily life in the context of the big picture." They can "deal with the threat in a constructive way, rather than spend mental energy on avoidance, suppression, and rationalization."

Social psychologist Robert Livingston applies these findings directly to conversations about identity. When you know such a conversation is going to happen, Livingston suggests you write down three self-affirmations beforehand. Those three things don't need to relate to the subject of the conversation. The point is not to neutralize the specific threat you're facing but to stabilize your overall sense of self. The affirmations could be about your most important relationships, your recent professional accomplishments, or the personal qualities that you value in yourself, like having a sense of humor or being generous. Livingston stresses that study after study has shown the benefits of engaging in self-affirmation before you enter situations involving self-threat. As he notes, "a more secure and happy person is a more tolerant person." The impending doom you sometimes feel in these conversations will abate when you're buoyed by a sense of self-worth.

Were we training you to run a marathon, we'd fuel you up with the right food. As we send you into identity conversations, we want you to have psychological fuel. Of course, you won't always have the opportunity to prepare for a conversation. Yet even in the throes of one, you can still try to calm the emotional storm by reminding yourself what matters most in your life. Chances are, "ensuring this conversation goes smoothly for me" won't be one of them.

### Right-Size Feedback

Imagine you're sitting across from your boss at your annual review. How would you feel if they told you: "You need to improve your organizational skills"? Feedback experts Douglas Stone and Sheila Heen suggest you'd probably blow it out of proportion. You might hear the statement as: "You're a terrible employee who will never get promoted." One antidote to that tendency is the growth mindset we've discussed. Another is what Stone and Heen call seeing feedback at "actual size." This means "finding ways to turn down the volume on that ominous soundtrack playing in our minds so that we can hear the dialogue more clearly."

Conversations about identity rarely involve formal performance evaluations. (Thank goodness.) Yet they constantly involve feedback on who you are or what you've done—whether it's a reference to your "privilege," a charge that you're "racist" or "sexist" or "homophobic," or a suggestion that something you did was offensive or harmful. You should right-size feedback in identity conversations by making sure what you're hearing is what the other person is saying.

To take a common example, imagine someone reminds you of your "white privilege," "male privilege," or whatever forms of privilege you have. How do you interpret the word "privilege"? If you're like many people we work with, you might hear it to suggest your life has been easy. As journalist Reni Eddo-Lodge states, the term can evoke an image of "life lived in the lap of luxury, enjoying the spoils of the super-rich." Think of the filthy rich characters in *Succession* or *Downton Abbey*. When Jennifer Gates, daughter of billionaires Bill and Melinda, says, "I was born into a huge situation of privilege," she's alluding to that sense of the term.

You might recoil from the idea that all lights turned green for you down the highway of life simply because you belong to certain social groups. We get it, because we do too, and so do many others. When we rolled out an employee survey for a tech company, one respondent complained that at work he's "expected to just be okay" because he's a white man. "How messed up is that?" he asked. Conservative writer Matt Walsh makes this point even more starkly: "Consider a white child living in a trailer in Clay

County, Kentucky. He lives in one of the poorest parts of the country, with perhaps the worst quality of life, and one of the highest suicide, overdose, and drop-out rates. Where does 'white privilege' come into play for him?"

Yet when people talk about your privilege, they don't usually mean your life has been a breeze. More typically, they mean you're privileged along a particular dimension of life. To name just a few of those possible dimensions, you have class privilege if you grew up in a wealthy family, citizenship privilege if you're a citizen of your country of residence, sexual orientation privilege if you're heterosexual, and ability privilege if you don't need a mobility aid to move around.

Because privilege is multidimensional, a person could have white privilege and male privilege while also having other severe disadvantages. We agree with Walsh that the white child living in a trailer is absolutely not privileged overall. But the child's race isn't one of his hardships. To answer Walsh's question squarely, the white child has race-based privilege compared to a Black child in a similar trailer.

A related misunderstanding occurs when you hear a reference to your privilege as a claim you've made no effort in your life. In an essay in *Time*, "Why I'll Never Apologize for My White Male Privilege," college student Tal Fortgang condemned those who told him to check his privilege. He chastised them for "diminishing everything I have personally accomplished, all the hard work I have done in my life, and for ascribing all the fruit I reap not to the seeds I sow but to some invisible patron saint of white maleness who places it out for me before I even arrive."

Again, this reaction might indicate a failure to hear feedback at actual size. When someone refers to your privilege, they're rarely if ever suggesting that "everything" you've accomplished or "all" your hard work can be reduced to privilege. The claim is that in addition to your talents and hard work, you've benefited from some invisible boosts in a way that someone who worked equally hard hasn't.

Some writers and scholars draw an analogy between privilege and tailwinds. Suppose you fly from east to west and then back again. The flight east will be faster because the jet stream supplies a tailwind on eastbound flights. Without feeling any difference, you'll arrive at your destination more quickly than when you fly west against a headwind. Social identities and life experiences can provide analogous tailwinds, allowing you to reach life destinations—such as stable housing, a good education, or a promotion at work—more easily. It doesn't mean the journey required no effort. It just means the journey required less effort than if you'd been flying against a headwind the whole time.

Conversations about privilege aren't the only place these misunderstandings arise. Another common and consequential mix-up occurs when people are accused of bias. Journalist Celeste Headlee, a self-described "light-skinned Black Jew," used to live in what had historically been an all-white community two blocks from the border with Detroit, a majority-Black city. Her older white male neighbor asked Headlee to collect his mail while he went on vacation. "I don't want those people," he said, gesturing toward Detroit, "to know that I'll be away." Headlee responded: "I'm happy to get your mail. But just so you know, I'm Black, so I'm one of those people." He immediately protested, "No, no, I'm not racist!" Headlee cheerfully corrected him: "You absolutely are. But I'm still going to get your mail, don't worry. Have a great vacation."

Many people might find it jarring to hear "You're racist" and "Have a great vacation" uttered in the same breath. As United

States Senator John Kennedy said: "It hurts to be called a racist. I think it's one of the worst things you can call an American." Yet Headlee clearly didn't mean the word "racist" in the sense of a card-carrying white supremacist. "If someone suggests that you are prejudiced," she says, "the most accurate response is 'Yes, you're right. I am.' Because the truth is that everyone is biased. Everyone."

Headlee is not alone. Here's Ijeoma Oluo: "If you are white in a white supremacist society, you are racist. If you are male in a patriarchy, you are sexist. If you are able-bodied, you are ableist. If you are anything above poverty in a capitalist society, you are classist." Is Oluo saying all white individuals are torch-wielding Klanspeople or all men are virulent misogynists? No. She's just saying it's impossible to live in a biased society without bias seeping into your beliefs and actions. It would be a miracle if you didn't internalize what psychologist Beverly Daniel Tatum calls cultural "smog," in the same way that someone who breathed in environmental smog every day would be a medical miracle if they had no traces of it in their lungs. On this understanding of bias, a person who perceives an assertive woman as "bossy" but perceives an equivalently assertive man as "confident" is sexist. No hostility toward women is required.

This way of talking about bias is still unfamiliar to many people. If that's true of you, you might hear the statement "I think you're racist" as the claim: "I think you, *unlike* most people in this society, are racist." But it may be the claim: "I think you, *like* most people in this society, are racist." Because of this misunderstanding, identity conversations can resemble slow-motion car crashes.

We increasingly notice this confusion across generational divides. Terms that older people reserve for conscious or individual forms of bias are now used by younger people to refer to uncon-scious or systemic forms of bias. Our friend Rhonda, a fierce advo-cate of diversity and inclusion in her early fifties, received a letter from junior employees who'd recently entered her creative arts or-ganization, urging her and other senior leaders to make changes to the workplace. The letter used terms like "white supremacy" and "racial violence" that sounded like accusations of rank bigotry. Rhonda was bewildered by the strength of the language and asked us for our take on the document. We sensed from our experience reading similar communications that the words were open to many interpretations, including that the leaders were unconsciously bi-ased like everyone else.

Sure enough, Rhonda spoke with the employees directly and found the dialogue less antagonistic than she had feared. They weren't accusing her and the other leaders of bigotry. Rather, they were bruised from bad experiences in previous jobs, and wanted assurances Rhonda's organization would be different. The employ-ees had a productive discussion with Rhonda about which work-place reforms were feasible and which ones weren't. Rhonda told them it was her job to create an inclusive work environment and said she welcomed more conversations to make sure she was deliv-ering on that responsibility.

We think Rhonda handled this situation impressively. Instead of assuming that the most extreme and personal interpretation of the employee feedback was correct, she sought out the employees to clarify what they meant. Sometimes in these conversations, a person's choice of words has less to do with you personally and more to do with accumulated experiences that diversity consul-tant Lily Zheng likens to shaking a can of soda. You might be sur-prised when a seemingly small incident makes the can explode, but you didn't witness all the prior incidents that caused the pressure to build to a breaking point. We think you can save yourself a lot of grief if, like Rhonda, you mind the gap between the other person's words and your interpretation of them. Hearing feedback at actual size will give you the space to process and learn from it.

## Name and Reframe Your Discomfort

The animated film *Inside Out* depicts the emotional life of a young girl named Riley in the most literal terms. Five personified emotions live in a control room in her mind: Joy, Sadness, Disgust, Fear, and Anger. The movie brilliantly depicts how each can take over in ways that dictate Riley's actions. While the vivid emotions can't be perceived by those on the "outside," they're running the show from the "inside."

When the film became a blockbuster hit, educators started to use it with children to help them identify their own emotions. After all, it's not only other people who can't perceive Riley's emotions—Riley herself doesn't see the little characters in her brain. A slew of teacher's guides and YouTube videos cropped up to make the point that she, and we, would all be better off if we could name what we're feeling.

Psychologists validate this pop intuition. Merely identifying the difficult emotions you're experiencing can reduce their harmful effects. Researchers aren't sure exactly why. Labeling your emotions might distract you from feeling them as strongly. It might also reduce the needling pain of uncertainty. Or it could disable the alarm system in your brain by engaging a different region of it. For whatever reason, as psychologist Marc Schoen puts it, "when you identify and describe your discomfort, you lessen the fears associated with it."

So when a wave of discomfort crashes over you in one of these conversations, pause and ask yourself what emotion you're feeling and why. In our experience, the dominant ones are fear, anger, guilt, and hopelessness.

Of the four dominant emotions, we think fear is the most common. In a study of university students, researchers asked participants to complete a test of "implicit racism" and told them their scores would be publicized (along with their names and majors) to everyone at the university. Before broadcasting the scores, however, researchers offered participants an escape hatch. If they didn't want their scores publicized, they could submerge their hand into a bucket of live worms for a full minute and let the worms crawl over them. Another group of participants were offered a less disgusting alternative of plunging their hands into a "pain machine" filled with nearly freezing water until they couldn't tolerate the agony. The test was rigged to give some participants a score of ninety-seven, which indicated "extremely racist." Of those participants, almost a third chose the worms, and a clear majority chose the pain machine, over their scores being publicized. (For our part, Kenji would have chosen the worms; David would have chosen the pain machine.)

This study speaks to a pervasive fear in many identity conversations—the fear of being exposed to others as biased. A related terror is that of getting canceled. One parent spoke anonymously to the *New York Post* about their fear of openly opposing the "woke" curriculum at their children's school: "Everyone is still deathly afraid of speaking publicly. They're scared to even talk to their friends. What middle-aged white guy working in a bank would dare speak out? They'd be fired tomorrow."

Similarly, Joanne Lipman observes that many men "would be happy to join in the conversation" about gender issues, but don't because they're "terrified of saying something wrong." She cites a survey in which 74 percent of men said fear chilled them from being more supportive of women. We witnessed this fear early in the #MeToo movement. Colleagues in many different organizations told us some male leaders had retreated from mentoring or interacting socially with women outside work, because they feared blurting out something offensive and being accused of sexual harassment.

Let's say you've looked inside your own mind and fear isn't the character pulling the levers. It could instead be anger—anger that you've been misunderstood, denied credit for your good intentions, or smeared. Judy Morelock, a white college lecturer in Tennessee, was furious when she clashed with her Black student Kayla Parker over a test question that Parker thought "whitewashed" Black history. When challenged by Parker, Morelock allegedly tried to deflect to her own progressive credentials as "someone who has spent their entire life fighting for people of diversity." After Parker continued to press the point, Morelock targeted her in a series of threatening posts on Facebook. University officials removed Parker from the class and eventually fired Morelock. The next fall, Morelock physically assaulted Parker in a grocery store. What began as a conversation about a pop quiz ended with a professor in police custody.

If you flip anger, you'll often find guilt on the other side. Anger is when you believe an accusation of wrongdoing is unfair. Guilt is when you accept it's fair and turn blame on yourself. Diversity expert Vernā Myers describes this emotion in a law firm interaction. A litigation partner told Ty, an Asian scientist in the firm's patent department, to contact a client regarding an urgent matter. The instruction bewildered Ty, who wasn't a lawyer. After mulling it over, Ty realized the partner had confused him with another Asian employee, Jason. Ty called Jason to let him know. Jason then phoned the partner to clarify the assignment, politely noting he wasn't the person the partner had addressed earlier. The partner apologized. The real problem surfaced later: the partner started ignoring Jason during meetings and stopped assigning him work. It's likely the partner withdrew from guilt over his error. Yet that response only made the situation worse, as Jason then became worried about his future at the firm.

Finally, if it's not fear, anger, or guilt, it could be hopelessness. We once helped facilitate a mentoring program for a global entertainment company. By design, the mentors in the program were mostly white and their mentees were mostly Black. After the opening session, some Black mentees offered feedback that the mentors were speaking too much and needed to "share the mic." At the next session, the white leaders deliberately hung back. They then received a blizzard of criticism for being checked out. One mentee told them, "silence is violence." Many of the leaders expressed hopelessness, feeling they could never satisfy these competing demands. Several threatened to quit the program altogether.

Even this short survey underscores how a vague sense of discomfort spans a wide array of specific emotions. Suss out which one you're feeling and you'll reap huge rewards. Psychologist Kristin Neff gives an example of what naming sounds like: "I am aware that I am feeling hurt, insulted, and angry right now. I'm going to take a deep breath and pause before I start shouting accusations." If you don't stop to name what you're feeling, you'll be, as Neff puts it, "lost in the story" of the emotion. But when you name it, you can tame it. You'll feel that *you* are having the conversation, not that your emotion is having the conversation for you.

Naming your emotion allows you to reframe it. Consider how a shift in mindset could transform each of the emotional reactions we've discussed.

| EMOTION | INITIAL REACTION | REFRAMED RESPONSE |
|---|---|---|
| **Fear** | "I'm going to keep my mouth shut about the school curriculum, because if I speak, people will think I'm a bigot and cancel me." | "I'll share my views respectfully, and if people criticize me, I can handle it." |
| **Anger** | "This arrogant student is accusing me of being incompetent and racist! She must be stopped." | "I'm grateful to have a smart, passionate student who challenges my perspective based on experiences I don't share." |
| **Guilt** | "I'm a horrible person for mixing up two people just because they're both Asian." | "Everyone makes mistakes. I'll apologize, learn their names, and try to do better next time." |
| **Hopelessness** | "I can't win. If I talk, I'm told to 'share the mic' and if I don't, I'm told 'silence is violence.'" | "It's not contradictory to say I sometimes talk too much and at other times talk too little. While I can't please everyone, I can find a better balance." |

Notice how each shift conceives of the discomfort not as something to avoid at all costs, but as a learning opportunity. In other areas of life, such as parenting, exercise, or studying a new language, people know the activity will involve discomfort and they do it anyway, because it generates its own rewards—meaningful relationships, greater health, or a sense of accomplishment. The discomfort of identity conversations is no different. There's joy in the struggle here too: new capabilities, a greater sense of purpose, and deeper human connections.

Don't worry if you can't make these shifts in the heat of the moment. Remember the option of taking an off-ramp from the conversation. You can use the break time to name and reframe your emotions before taking an on-ramp to continue the dialogue. As you practice naming and reframing, you'll also develop the ability to do it more quickly and naturally.

We witnessed the power of reframing when we asked the white mentors at the entertainment company to identify their emotion after they were told to "share the mic" and then told "silence is violence." When they did, they then reframed the experience without any prompting on our part. "Even as I say I felt hopeless," one leader said, "it sounds ridiculous." He continued: "It's like saying we can't ever find the right room temperature because it was too hot the first day and too cold the next. Yes, it's hard to achieve an optimal balance of talking and listening, but I do hard things in my job all the time."

## Seek Appropriate Support

When clinical psychologist Susan Silk had breast cancer, a colleague insisted on visiting her after the surgery. Silk didn't want visitors, and said so. The colleague responded: "This isn't just about you." Silk was understandably floored: "My breast cancer is not about me? It's about you?"

Reflecting on that experience, Silk and her friend Barry Goldman, a mediator, developed "ring theory," a framework for anyone helping a person in crisis. Their instructions are simple: Draw a series of concentric rings. In the center circle, write the name of the person experiencing the harm. In the second circle out, write the names of those closest to that person—a spouse or partner, family members, or close friends. In the third circle out, include people another step removed. Draw as many circles as necessary to capture the ecosystem of individuals around the person in crisis.

The cardinal rule of ring theory is "comfort in, dump out." For the person in the center, everywhere is "out," so they can "dump out" their negative emotions to anyone. (This prerogative, the authors wryly note, is one of the few benefits of being at the center of a crisis.) Those who aren't in the center circle, however, need to be more careful. They should direct comfort inward, while directing their complaints, fears, and resentments outward. As someone in the second circle out, Silk's colleague shouldn't have "dumped in" her resentment about being unable to visit Silk. Critically, this framework didn't leave the colleague to fend for herself. She could have "dumped out" her feelings to, say, her own friends.

We've found the "dump out" rule in ring theory useful in conversations about identity. When you're speaking with someone about a form of hardship they're experiencing, think of them as being in the center circle, and yourself as being in the second circle out. You can express your negative feelings, but only to people in the outer circles:

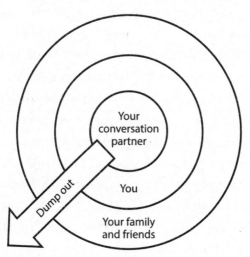

Many people violate this guideline. One common frustration for people of color is when white people cry in cross-racial interactions without realizing it could draw attention away from the person who needs it. Sometimes it's to deflect responsibility. As Arab Australian writer Ruby Hamad shares: "As I look back over my adult life a pattern emerges. Often, when I have attempted to speak to or confront a white woman about something she has said or done that has impacted me adversely, I am met with tearful denials and indignant accusations that I am hurting her." This maneuver, Hamad notes, turns the other woman into the victim and Hamad into the perpetrator: "My confidence diminished and second-guessing myself, I either flare up in frustration at not being heard (which only seems to prove her point) or I back down immediately, apologizing and consoling the very person causing me harm."

Author Adiba Jaigirdar had a similar experience when she formed a feminist discussion group with three friends soon after graduating college. As the only woman of color and only Muslim in the group, she frequently felt sidelined in their conversations. In one instance, a friend shared an article with the group that portrayed Muslim women as antifeminist. When Jaigirdar tried to offer a different perspective, the other women dismissed her. After repeated experiences like this one, Jaigirdar quit the group.

Months later, she shared with one of the women, Nathalie, how she felt "her experience and voice were devalued." Nathalie responded by crying and castigating herself for not noticing these issues at the time. She called herself a "bad friend" and "bad feminist." "Instead of spending time talking about the racism and Islamophobia I had dealt with," Jaigirdar observed, "the rest of our time together was spent with me trying to comfort and reassure." Jaigirdar ended the conversation feeling "even worse off."

Tears can also flow when an ally is moved by a poignant story and cries in solidarity. We've both cried in this manner before. But even here, the behavior can unhelpfully draw attention away from the substance of the conversation. Library assistant Jennifer Loubriel was discussing police brutality with a mixed group of white people and people of color. Loubriel notes that many of the people of color in the room were "having a very difficult time" discussing the topic: "It was a hard but healing kind of conversation." Then one of the white women in the room began to cry. The woman said police violence didn't affect her directly, but she was "having a hard time dealing with everything." "The tone of the conversation shifted," Loubriel observes. "Half of the people in the room went to comfort her. The other half, myself included, began to roll our eyes, cross our arms over our chests, and completely tune the discussion out."

We want to be careful in describing this issue. Bursting into tears is rarely a calculated performance. We aren't saying the only way to respond to hurt feelings is stoic silence. That being said, allies should remember the focal point of the conversation. If you cry and feel you're siphoning attention from the person who needs it most, then it seems wise—as professor and diversity consultant Robin DiAngelo suggests—to say and show you're able to take care of yourself.

Listening to someone with less privilege share experiences of bias and discrimination can be challenging, and you may accumulate a bunch of negative feelings. Conscious of the impact your emotions may have on the other person, you may decide to be a superhero and deal with the difficulties on your own. We don't recommend that approach.

Seeking support will not only benefit you by giving you an outlet for your own pain, but it will also make you a better ally to the other person. A study of white allies found that the more "social support" allies had from important people in their lives, the more involved they were in racial justice work. So put away that superhero cape and enlist support. You'll get help to process your feelings, and you'll build a community of allies who can strengthen each other whenever this work gets tough.

⊁⊜

You might be wondering what happened to Kenji's rage and David's guilt after our respective meetings.

We decided to take our own advice. Kenji followed ring theory and vented to a friend, who gently pointed out he'd fallen prey to the "hard-knock life effect" we discussed in Principle 1 (Beware the Four Conversational Traps) by deflecting from his privilege to his hardship. Kenji right-sized Alicia's feedback by remembering that Alicia didn't say he was privileged along all dimensions of life. She merely suggested Kenji had privilege in this context because his children weren't Black. Kenji named his emotion (anger) and reframed it to view the interaction differently: "I'm glad to have a colleague at the school who reminds me of gaps in my awareness. If anti-Asian or anti-LGBTQ+ bias occurs at the school, I know Alicia would want me to close any gaps in her awareness as well."

David also engaged in self-reflection in the days following his interaction with the professionals of color. He realized he was stuck in a fixed mindset, viewing any misstep in a conversation as a reflection of his moral character. He reminded himself that he, like everyone, was learning. He also reminded himself what really mattered in his life—his family, his friends, and the values that brought him to the work of diversity and inclusion in the first place. Following ring theory, David asked his husband for reassurance that it's human to feel guilt in these conversations. He obtained all the comfort he needed.

After getting support, we were able to stop working through our own emotional reactions and realize these incidents weren't really about us, but about our friends and colleagues. Kenji apologized to Alicia for not engaging with her on the issue she invited him to address, and pledged to be a better ally. David had already apologized in the first meeting, but made a commitment to himself to demonstrate better allyship through his actions. We haven't magically transformed our emotional responses in identity conversations, and to this day continue to experience bouts of fear, anger, guilt, or hopelessness. Yet the point is to keep engaging. In these instances, we've both gone on to hold many more productive and enriching conversations with the individuals who called us out. Emotionally resilient, we persevered.

## Principle 2 **TAKEAWAYS**

- You need strategies to manage the emotional discomfort triggered by identity conversations. While taking an "off-ramp" is a good start, it's often not enough on its own.

- Adopt a growth mindset by treating mistakes as opportunities to learn, rather than as judgments of your moral character.

- Self-affirm by reminding yourself what matters in your life, such as your most important relationships, core values, or accomplishments.

- Right-size feedback by remembering that claims about your privilege or your bias are often not as extreme and personal as you perceive them to be. If someone suggests you're racist, sexist, or biased in some other way, consider whether they meant it to refer to a subtle or unconscious form of bias.

- Name your specific emotional experience (such as fear, anger, guilt, or hopelessness) and try to reframe the situation so the emotion doesn't hold you captive.

- Seek support using "ring theory"—dump out your negative feelings, but not to your conversation partner.

# Principle 3:

# Cultivate Curiosity

S oon after the Oxford online dictionary added the term "mansplaining," author and "dating expert" Steve Santagati gave us a vivid demonstration of it. A viral video showed actor Shoshana Roberts walking the sidewalks of New York City through a sea of catcalling men. CNN invited Santagati to discuss the video alongside comedian Amanda Seales.

The anchor, Fredricka Whitfield, asked Seales to react to the footage. "I live this life every day," Seales said. "I think guys think that by letting you know that they would be interested in sleeping with you, that that is a compliment. And actually it's really just objectifying me when I'm trying to walk in my daily life." While Seales spoke, Santagati shook his head and interrupted her. Seales observed: "I can see you shaking your head, but you are not an expert on this, my brother, because you are not a woman walking in the street. So you don't know."

"I'm more of an expert than you," Santagati shot back. "I'm a guy, and I know how we think." He elaborated: "You would not care if all these guys were hot. They would be bolstering your self-esteem, bolstering your ego. There is nothing more that a woman loves to hear than how pretty she is." Santagati then challenged the video's authenticity: "I'm also very suspicious because this was put together by an ad agency to go viral, so how do we know some of those guys weren't planted?"

Seales responded: "It doesn't matter, because even if they were planted, this is actually very accurate for New York City." She highlighted Santagati's bait and switch: "What's funny is that you're saying that you know how men think, but actually your comment was about saying how women think." Santagati shot back: "Am I wrong? Stop me when I'm wrong." Seales replied: "You are wrong." Santagati refused to back down, insisting that the catcalls were "compliments."

At this point, Seales called Santagati out: "You really should just be embracing and welcoming to the fact that women are saying, 'Hey, we don't like this.' Not arguing why we shouldn't. If we say we don't like it, and we are demonstrating that, then you should actually . . . be saying, 'Well, let's discuss how we can make you all feel more comfortable.'" As she tried to elaborate, Santagati interrupted: "No, that's not going to happen." Soon after, Whitfield brought the conversation to a merciful close.

You've already seen how identity conversations can trigger strong emotional reactions. We started by offering tools for resilience, because it's hard to learn any other skill when you're flooded with negative emotions. Yet resilience isn't enough. Throughout the conversation, Santagati didn't appear fearful, angry, guilty, or hopeless. He seemed chipper, even jaunty, while still engaging in utterly cringeworthy behavior. He voiced his views definitively—

not as opinions but as facts. He refused to consider perspectives that differed from his own. And he failed to acknowledge that people with direct experience of the issue might have greater expertise.

This example is extreme, and you might be tempted to think, *I would never do that, so I'm off the hook.* But members of nondominant groups experience Santagati-like behavior all the time. Some of their most common frustrations relate to allies who don't know enough about the relevant issues, lack humility about gaps in their awareness, and don't take the perspectives of nondominant group members seriously enough. In truth, nearly every ally could benefit from being a little less self-assured and a little more curious.

## Increase Your Knowledge

When you play *Trivial Pursuit* with your friends, do you seem to get harder questions than they do? When the season schedules are released, does your favorite football team seem to get the short end of the stick? Assuming you have a sibling, when you think back to your childhood, did your parents spoil your sibling more than they spoiled you?

If your answers to these questions are yes, you're in good company. Psychologists Shai Davidai and Thomas Gilovich have found a "headwinds/tailwinds asymmetry," meaning that people notice their headwinds (disadvantages) much more than their tailwinds (advantages). In their study, participants asked to compete in a trivia contest were much more likely to remember their opponents' trivia categories as being easy, even when both sides were given comparable questions. Football fans were twice as likely to focus on their team's disadvantages in the season schedule than their advantages. Adults more easily recalled moments from their childhood when their parents favored their sibling than when their parents favored them. As Davidai and Gilovich conclude: "Tailwinds and blessings can be enjoyed and ignored without being fully attended to. Headwinds and barriers, in contrast, need to be overcome, and therefore command our attention."

Because of this imbalance in what people notice, members of less privileged groups come to identity conversations with knowledge that more privileged people generally haven't needed to learn. Suppose your conversation partner has a motor disability and uses a wheelchair. They'll know which parts of their neighborhood have curb cuts or ramps, and which parts are challenging or impossible to navigate. They'll know what biases wheelchair users encounter as they go about their lives, what strategies work (or don't) to counteract those biases, and what accommodations they need to use public amenities on equal terms. They'll also intimately understand the ways of the dominant group—the expectations, assumptions, prejudices, and values of nondisabled people—because they have to stay on good terms with dominant group members. In contrast, if you don't have a motor disability, you'll know less about these subjects unless you've immersed yourself in disability culture.

For this reason, less privileged individuals also tend to perceive identity dimensions of everyday interactions that more privileged individuals don't see. During the COVID-19 pandemic, HR managers in several organizations told us that administrative assistants were logging in to virtual meetings from cramped apartments with spotty internet connections. Feeling self-conscious, many assistants hid their environment with virtual backgrounds. Some senior leaders weren't so coy. They dialed in from exotic locations like the Bahamas, or from the grounds of their second homes with views of their stately mansions behind them. To many of the leaders, these meetings were unremarkable. To many of the assistants, they were pointed reminders of class inequality. "The leaders don't realize how they're making their assistants feel," one HR manager told us.

In a study of college students, researchers discovered the same gap between what students from lower and upper socioeconomic backgrounds noticed. "For first-generation college students," the researchers observed, "ostensibly mundane, day-to-day situations and institutional contexts" were "glaring reminders of class differences." Students from low-income backgrounds noticed that socioeconomically privileged students studied in cafés while those with less privilege studied in the library. They also noticed class differences in the laptops students used, the cars they drove, the clothing they wore, and how they interacted with workers at campus stores. Upper-income students, however, appeared oblivious. According to the researchers, these students "failed to notice these same status symbols and expressed little or no awareness of or sensitivity to what their peers from the lower social classes might be experiencing." Some reported that "they did not really see any social class differences on campus." Tellingly, the one student from a high socioeconomic background who was sensitive to these differences had "intentionally cultivated diverse friendships."

We're not blaming you for having less knowledge about areas where you experience a tailwind. When you hold more power in society, you don't need to know much about less powerful groups to live comfortably, so there's no built-in incentive to learn. Now, however, you have a new incentive—to be a good ally. And good allies exhibit curiosity.

You can begin by teaching yourself the issues. You'll never be able to fully imagine your way into another person's experience, so significant knowledge gaps will always remain. At the same time, you can acquire a lot of the knowledge you need through books, articles, podcasts, documentaries, or conversations with other allies. The effort you make to learn will fill gaps in your understanding so you enter conversations more aware at the outset. It will also lead you to be less surprised by what you hear in conversation. You won't dismiss as many viewpoints just because they're unfamiliar.

To get started, look for mainstream organizations that educate the public on particular identities. Expecting a conversation about Sikhism? No problem: the Sikh Coalition publishes an online guide to the religion, including its history, core beliefs and practices, and biases that Sikhs frequently encounter. What about a conversation on intersex identity? Again, the Intersex Campaign for Equality has a web page with articles, book suggestions, and guidelines for allies to the intersex community.

Make sure to do some quality control. In debates on topics such as trans rights and anti-bullying programs in schools, opponents of LGBTQ+ rights sometimes cite the American College of Pediatricians to support their positions. When we first came across these citations, we were surprised an organization that sounded so credible would take such strong stances against LGBTQ+ rights. Sure enough, a quick search revealed it was a small splinter group that broke off from the mainstream body of pediatric physicians—the American Academy of Pediatrics—to protest the academy's support of same-sex parenting. Mystery solved.

This level of research might sound labor-intensive. A corporate leader once asked us while literally pulling on her own hair: "I'm incredibly busy—do I really have to read all these books?" We have a gentle and a stern answer to this question. The gentle answer is that the necessary information—What's a land acknowledgment? What does neurodiverse mean? Is pansexual different from bisexual?—is often a mouse click away. Ijeoma Oluo offers pithy advice: "If we have to live it, the least you can do is Google it." The stern answer is, well, yes, if you want to improve at having conversations about identity, you need to read the books, watch the documentaries, or listen to the podcasts. Imagine saying you want to learn a new language but don't want to read or listen to it.

You may have noticed we left out "people affected by bias" as a resource to consult. Please be careful here. For starters, affected people may not have the expertise you think they do. Just because someone has a particular identity doesn't mean they're expert in all matters even vaguely touching on that identity. Uma Narayan, an Indian philosopher who works in the United States, observes: "I have, in my fairly short span of time as an academic, been consulted by students working on Indian novels in English, the role of women in popular Hindi films, and Goddess-worship rituals in South India, none of which remotely fall into my realms of academic expertise." Students from underrepresented groups frequently tell us they feel pressure to be a "spokesperson" when an issue related to their identity comes up in the classroom. They're expected to offer the "immigrant perspective," the "Muslim perspective," or the "trans perspective." In Principle 1 (Beware the Four Conversational Traps), we warned against pretending you can't see a person's identity. In this context, be careful not to overcorrect by ignoring their individuality. One person's experience cannot be the universal experience.

Even if you limit your questions to areas within someone's expertise, you can overload them. During the protests of summer 2020, a Black colleague of ours compared speaking with white people at that time to "having forty friends wake up from a four-hundred-year coma wanting to be briefed." Black writer Damon Young found such outreach intolerable. He explained how white neighbors stopped him during his strolls through the neighborhood to share how they had been "thinking about everything happening in the country" and to discuss "what white people can do" about racism. Young quipped: "I doubt the Road Runner, after a day of outrunning, outscheming and outlasting Wile E. Coyote, wishes to come home and explain coyote supremacy to the liberal coyotes who live in his neighborhood."

The late-night comedy program *The Daily Show*, with Trevor Noah, offered a solution to this problem: the "Blacklexa" gadget. In a satirical advertisement, the narrator asks: "Are you tired of your white friends interrupting your busy day with questions about race relations?" It then introduces the Blacklexa, a play on the voice-based digital assistant Alexa. The ad shows Blacklexa tackling questions from white customers, such as "I'm confused. What's wrong with saying 'All Lives Matter'?" and "I want to go to a protest, but I don't know how to chant." The narrator mischievously observes that the device will "absorb all the emotional labor of helping your well-meaning but painfully white pals." Yet by the end of the parody, even Blacklexa is exhausted: "I need a new job."

As always, our guideline not to ask someone to teach you about their identity is just that—a guideline rather than an absolute rule. Some members of affected groups are comfortable, even pleased, to educate you. You'll want to consider factors like the individual's role and personality, your relationship to them, and the type of knowledge you seek.

Sometimes the person *wants* to bridge the gap between their experience and yours. These are the translators and teachers of the world, whether they officially hold those titles or not. In our lifetimes, countless straight people have asked us about aspects of gay identity and culture. If the questions are appropriate to the context and posed in a genuine spirit of learning, we're generally happy to answer them. But we're teachers by vocation and temperament. Not everyone is.

It's also critical to distinguish between people you know well and people you don't. We're obviously willing to have intimate conversations with close friends. Yet when random people at an airport ask a battery of questions about our children—"How did you have them?" "Surrogacy or adoption?" "Who's biologically related to whom?"—we feel a sudden urge to live off the grid as yeoman farmers. If in doubt, "asking to ask" can help. A simple phrase like "If you don't mind my asking . . ." or "Let me know if this is too personal, but I'm wondering . . ." goes a long way.

Finally, think about the type of information. Questions that don't intrude on someone's privacy are much more likely to be well received. People with disabilities and transgender people routinely get invasive questions: "What happened to you?" "How do you have sex?" "Have you had surgery?" "What about hormones?" Remember that if you're asking, many others are too. So imagine how exhausting it would be to get flooded with these inquiries.

Now you have some guidance on how to increase your knowledge and some pitfalls to avoid. You might be wondering when you've learned enough. If, as a male ally, you're trying to learn about women's rights and you've read Roxane Gay, do you also need to add Betty Friedan, Audre Lorde, and Janet Mock to your reading list? What about Catharine MacKinnon and bell hooks? When does it end?

In a world awash with information, don't let the sense of overload freeze you into doing nothing. Instead, you can scale the effort to the intervention. You don't need to have studied feminist icons to know it's wrong for your brother to make a sexist comment at the dinner table—you can speak up with the knowledge you have. (For tips on how to do that, see Principle 7 (Be Generous to the Source).) But if you want to organize a panel for International Women's Day at your college, or suggest changes to your company's recruitment processes to improve gender equity, you should invest more time.

We promise you: even a modest effort to increase your knowledge will make you a more confident and more effective ally to the people you want to support. It will also help ensure that when you do have questions, you won't be asking your conversation partner to educate you. You'll be asking for their perspective on something about which you've begun to educate yourself.

## Adopt a Learning Posture

In an episode of the TV series *Fashion Police*, white entertainment reporter Giuliana Rancic commented on the appearance of Black actor Zendaya. Referring to Zendaya's dreadlocks, Rancic noted: "I feel like she smells like patchouli oil . . . and weed." Zendaya responded by observing that Rancic's remark was "not only a large stereotype but outrageously offensive." She added: "There is already a harsh criticism of African American hair in society without the help of ignorant people who choose to judge others based on the curl of their hair."

Initially, Rancic dismissed Zendaya's reference to race: "I was referring to a bohemian chic look. Had NOTHING to do with race and NEVER would!!!" Soon after, however, Rancic concluded that her reflexive reaction was grounded in ignorance. In an on-air apology, she stated: "This really has been a learning experience for me. I've learned a lot today and this incident has taught me to be a lot more aware of clichés and stereotypes, how much damage they can do."

A white person who had adopted our first strategy and in-

creased their knowledge on the subject of anti-Black racism probably could have avoided Rancic's error at the outset. As Zendaya
suggested, Black individuals have experienced a long history of
discrimination for their natural hair or for styles like braids, corn-
rows, and dreadlocks. Some U.S. states have even outlawed discrimination on the basis of hair as a form of race discrimination.
But we're more interested in Rancic's knee-jerk insistence that
her comment "had NOTHING to do with race." It seems not just
that Rancic *didn't know* her comment had racial undertones. She
also *didn't know that she didn't know.* To her, the remark about
"patchouli oil and weed" was just playful teasing.

In the TV comedy *The Big Bang Theory*, the character Howard
tells his friend Sheldon that he's wrong about something. Sheldon
responds: "Howard, you know me to be a very smart man. Don't
you think if I were wrong, I'd know it?" Well, it turns out Sheldon
was wrong about at least that. As former United States secretary
of defense Donald Rumsfeld famously remarked, ignorance comes
in different forms: the "known unknowns" (where you know you
don't know something) and the "unknown unknowns" (where you
don't know about your own ignorance).

In identity conversations, you might know you don't really understand the difference between the terms "transgender," "nonbinary," "genderqueer," "genderfluid," and "agender." But at least you
can correct your ignorance because you're aware it exists—it's a
known unknown. The more troubling form of ignorance relates
to the unknown unknowns. You might think you grasp what it
means to be transgender, yet have no clue someone can be transgender without taking hormones or undergoing gender confirma-
tion surgery. Because you're not aware of this form of ignorance,
you'll have a harder time overcoming it.

Sometimes unknown unknowns aren't a big deal: you make

an unwitting error, someone corrects you, and you apologize and move on. Other times, however, unknown unknowns lead people to be as overconfident as Steve Santagati, swaggering into a conversation on the assumption they already know enough.

An example here is the common "this isn't about . . ." gambit, where someone flatly denies a conversation is about identity without considering whether they have the necessary knowledge to make that assessment. Think of statements like "Don't make this about race," "Don't play the gender card," or Rancic's own statement that her comment "had NOTHING to do with race and NEVER would!!!" even after someone from an affected group suggested otherwise.

In his groundbreaking work *Thinking, Fast and Slow*, psychologist and economist Daniel Kahneman points out that people tend to build their view of the world based on the limited information in front of them. They then tend to treat such limited information "as if it were all there is to know." Robert Livingston, the psychologist who taught us about self-affirmation, ran into this dynamic when he asked an audience of white men to guess how many Fortune 500 CEOs were Black. One guessed seventy-five to eighty, another guessed a hundred, while still another guessed a hundred and fifty. The answer? Five. The audience couldn't believe it. They based their guesses on the limited information they saw in front of them. "When I turn on the TV, I see Obama, Oprah, Jay-Z, Beyoncé, all these rich and famous Black people," one participant said.

You might assume a person's confidence would rise in lock-step with their knowledge, so that the best-informed people would be the most sure of themselves. If only! The reverse is frequently true. Researchers have discovered a "beginner's bubble" where people develop an inflated sense of their expertise as they start to acquire new knowledge. With just "a little learning," one study observes, "beginners quickly come to believe they know much if not all there is to know."

How can you avoid this overconfidence? Take philosopher Kristie Dotson's approach and imagine you're about to attend a class on nuclear physics. Unless you're a nuclear physicist, you'll probably enter the class sharply aware of your ignorance. Even if you study the assigned readings and familiarize yourself with the topic beforehand, you may still feel intimidated by the complexity of the subject. In some ways, your prep work for the class might make you feel better informed. In other ways, it might alert you to the vast knowledge you still lack.

Dotson notes that she'd be able to "comprehend some portions" of a nuclear physics lecture, but she'd "always be on guard" for lapses in her understanding. Because of that vigilance, she'd be much more likely to detect when she was not "getting it" and know when she needed to ask more questions. And even if she felt she understood the material, she'd still be wary: "I may think to myself, 'I wonder if I understand this correctly.'"

Of course, as we've emphasized, your conversation partner probably isn't a subject-matter expert on all issues related to their group identity, so don't treat them like a professor. Nonetheless, we think Dotson's learning posture is helpful. No matter how much time you've spent increasing your knowledge, you'll always come to identity conversations with unknown unknowns. That means you should enter them keenly aware of your cognitive limitations and vigilant that you may need to ask more questions to really "get it." Specifically, you'll need to listen generously and share tentatively.

On the listening side, respect the extra knowledge the other person brings to the conversation. You might think: *That statement doesn't seem right to me, but let me keep an open mind, because*

*I know less about this topic.* On the sharing side, a learning posture will make you express your own views more cautiously, testing them with your own skepticism and the skepticism of the other person. When you're tempted to assert that something *is* or *isn't* a certain way, replace it with an "I" statement so that statements of fact become statements of personal perception: "I think . . . ," "I feel . . . ," "I wonder . . ." Some call this tentative approach "speaking in drafts." We often make this posture explicit in our own conversations: "Here's my reaction to what you said, but it's a draft, so please edit it."

This conversational style can feel unnatural to some allies. Members of advantaged social groups are often more accustomed to speaking than listening. One study divided participants into pairs and asked each of them to have a "get-acquainted interaction" for five minutes. The researchers found that people from high socioeconomic backgrounds showed more nonverbal signs of disengagement than people from low socioeconomic backgrounds. They were more likely to "self-groom, fidget with nearby objects, and doodle" during the conversation, rather than listening attentively to their conversation partners. This finding accorded with other studies the researchers cited, which found that high-power individuals tended to "focus their gaze less on other people," were "more likely to interrupt," and tended "to speak at greater length" than low-power individuals.

You might have to work hard to overcome these ingrained tendencies to speak more than you listen. Over time, though, we think you'll find it liberating to listen generously and share tentatively, because you'll stop feeling pressure to claim greater knowledge than you have. Although we've emphasized the dangers of silence, this area is one where measured silence, punctuated by thoughtful questions, can serve you well. Rather than communicating indifference, listening carefully to the other person and showing an interest in their viewpoint will signal that you're an engaged ally.

This conversational technique is such a simple yet powerful solution that we despair at how frequently people make unforced errors that they could have avoided by communicating their opinions cautiously. Imagine how much better Rancic would have fared had she replaced her statement that her comment "had NOTHING to do with race and NEVER would!!!" with: "I'm having trouble seeing the race dimensions of my comment but I may be missing something. I'm curious to learn why my remark landed the way it did." Other statements like "don't play the gender card" could become questions: "From your perspective, where does gender come into play here?"

More systematically, you can set the table for any given conversation with a statement of humility. We often begin identity conversations by saying some version of "I'm still learning here," or "I don't have this all figured out," to signal that we're in a learning posture. No matter how ignorant you may feel in these discussions, your conversation partner will appreciate you for having one piece of critical knowledge that many allies don't: you know there are things you don't know.

## Interrupt the Running Commentary of Skepticism

In a classic cartoon, five men and one woman are sitting around a conference-room table having a business meeting. The woman has just contributed something to the discussion. The man at the head of the table responds: "That's an excellent suggestion, Miss Triggs. Perhaps one of the men here would like to make it."

In a story in the *New York Times*, a former employee of a large independent bookseller describes the same dynamic: "Often, a suggestion made by one of the female staff during meetings the owner attended would be shot down, only to reappear in a week or two as his own brilliant idea." Some employees even joked about using a calendar to see how many days "it would take for our ideas to go from ridiculously impossible to sheer genius." Many of our clients tell us this phenomenon happens regularly in their workplaces too—it's as if a woman's word is on a 25 percent discount relative to her male peers.

Philosopher Miranda Fricker calls this dynamic "testimonial injustice," an unfairness that "occurs when prejudice causes a hearer to give a deflated level of credibility to a speaker's word." Fricker's colleague Linda Martín Alcoff provides an example in a white male teaching assistant who made baseless complaints against an untenured Chicana professor. When the professor raised this issue with her colleagues, they didn't believe her. Later, a senior white male professor had the same experience with the teaching assistant, which led the rest of the faculty to change their view and rally around the Chicana professor. Fricker points out that this junior professor encountered testimonial injustice twice—once from the student who didn't credit her expertise, and again from her colleagues. While this particular professor benefited from the happenstance that a senior colleague backed up her view, that won't always be the case. And regardless, as Alcoff observes, the Chicana professor "suffered two years of anguish and self-doubt because of this roadblock in her career."

Once you know the concept of testimonial injustice, we think you'll spot it everywhere. Women and people of color tend to receive less medical attention than their male or white counterparts when they report pain. Women entrepreneurs are less likely to persuade investors to fund their business ventures, even when they make the same pitches as men. Testimonial injustice can also lead people to mistrust a group's claim about its very existence. Bisexuals are often viewed as people who don't have the courage to come out as gay. Trans people are sometimes considered mistaken about their own identities because they're supposedly confused or mentally ill.

It's not only that people with less privilege suffer what Fricker calls a "credibility deficit," but also that people with more privilege are granted a "credibility excess." Just as someone with a working-class British accent may be taken less seriously than they deserve, someone with a posh British accent may be taken more seriously than they deserve. A federal judge once told us that even though she's a feminist, she has to fight her own tendency to think tall white male lawyers with deep voices sound more authoritative.

You might discount someone's testimony not only because of who they are, but also because of what they say. In discussions of identity, diversity, and justice, your conversation partner will often make statements that challenge the status quo. If you benefit from the current social order, it can be difficult to fully accept that the system isn't fair. You might unconsciously look for reasons to reject the other person's viewpoint. As writer Upton Sinclair noted: "It is difficult to get a man to understand something, when his salary depends upon his not understanding it." Privilege can function a bit like a salary.

We call the self-talk associated with this discounting the "running commentary of skepticism." Here's what it looks like in action. In an interview with researchers, a white college student described her internal monologue when people of color spoke to her about racial discrimination: "A Chinese lady says that her party had to wait longer while Whites kept getting seated in front of them. I say other people had made reservations. A Black man says that the receptionist was rude, and made him wait longer because he's Black. I say she had a bad day." Admirably self-aware, the student acknowledged that while she was "listening with a sympathetic ear," she continued to offer up "benign explanations that kept my world in equilibrium." Given that people rarely come out and say, "I am discriminating against you because of your social identity," such benign explanations will nearly always be available to you, which means you have to guard against them.

We think the running commentary of skepticism hugely disadvantages nondominant groups, because it goes over and above the healthy skepticism people can and should apply in ordinary conversations. It's as if the more privileged party is watching the other person speak on TV about unfair hardship with a news ticker scrolling by underneath them that reads "MAYBE IT WAS A MISUNDERSTANDING" or "MAYBE THEY'RE NOT REMEMBERING THE INCIDENT CORRECTLY."

It's important to understand the harm the running commentary of skepticism causes to the other side of the conversation. Reni Eddo-Lodge describes the massive resistance she meets when she tries to discuss structural racism with white people: "It's like something happens to the words as they leave our mouths and reach their ears. The words hit a barrier of denial and they don't get any further." Eddo-Lodge goes on to report what that barrier of denial has done to her: "I cannot continue to emotionally exhaust myself trying to get this message across." Then comes the kicker: "I'm no longer talking to white people about race. I don't have a huge amount of power to change the way the world works, but I can set boundaries." Over time, your running commentary of skepticism can make the other person give up in frustration and stop speaking to you about identity issues at all.

To overcome the tendency to discount less privileged speakers,

Fricker has a suggestion. She says to consider what weight you're assigning someone else's comment, understand that your assessment is affected by prejudice, and then adjust the weight. If you think you're discounting a woman's word by 25 percent, mentally bump her back up. While Fricker acknowledges no "algorithm" can determine precisely what weight to assign, she argues the "guiding ideal" is clear.

We agree that it helps to pause and question your gut reaction when you're inclined to dismiss someone's perspective. As with all unconscious biases, the running commentary of skepticism crops up most when you're on autopilot. Shifting gears from reflexive mode to reflective mode will enable you to catch yourself.

We recommend a couple of ways to make this gear shift. One is to flip the object of your skepticism from the other person to yourself. Suppose you're a man listening to a woman and you think her perspective sounds bizarre. In that situation, philosopher Louise Antony suggests you adopt a "working hypothesis" that it is *you* who doesn't understand, not the other way around. We like the idea of a "working hypothesis" because it doesn't mean you totally defer to a position that could be wrong. Rather, you give the other person a fair chance to be heard.

The other strategy is to imagine how you'd react if instead of hearing the story from a less privileged person, you heard it from a more privileged one. Let's say a Muslim woman tells you someone hurled an Islamophobic slur at her while she was walking to work, and your skeptical mind thinks she probably misheard the comment or is exaggerating how bad it was. Stop and imagine how you'd react if a non-Muslim man told you he witnessed the same incident. If you're more likely to believe him than her, that moment of realization can help you break down the running commentary of skepticism the next time you hear a story of bias or discrimination. You don't need to believe everything you hear in an identity conversation. But your conversation partner shouldn't have to work extra hard just to be taken seriously.

⟡

Our friend Helen, a white woman, is a university administrator in a student-facing role. Her decades of experience at the college had led her to believe the institution showed equal concern for all students. Yet as she skimmed the results of a recent "climate survey" about the campus culture, her confidence was shaken. Students of color had reported vastly more incidents of racism than she had anticipated. Helen stopped skimming and started poring over each page. She felt shock, and a faint pang of disbelief. The results seemed out of step with the open and inclusive culture she and other administrators had worked tirelessly to build.

Helen reached out to the survey designer, Darius, and asked to meet him to discuss the results. They met outside her office building. "The survey findings surprised me," she said to him. "We're a liberal college. I meet with students every day. I don't hear about all the racism that jumps off the pages of your survey. What am I missing?"

Darius, who is a large Black man, told Helen to stay where she was on the sidewalk for a moment. "I'm going to walk over there," he said, gesturing at the intersection ahead. "And I'm going to do it twice. The first time, I'll walk by myself. I want you to notice the white people walking toward me on the same side of the street and see what they do." "The second time," Darius added, "I'm going to walk with you beside me, and I want you to see if it makes a difference."

Helen waited on the sidewalk. As Darius walked on his own, one white person after another crossed the street as soon as they saw him approaching. They felt intimidated by his mere presence on the sidewalk. "Now let's do it together," Darius said. As they walked side by side, Helen noticed a startling shift. The passersby all stayed on the same side of the street. Accompanied by a white woman, Darius automatically seemed less frightening to them. "This is what I live every day," Darius told her.

Helen teared up as she realized her perception of the campus climate had been shaped by her own perspective. She didn't know about the extent of the racial bias on campus, and even more important, she didn't know that she didn't know. It was a humbling reminder that even as a stalwart ally on issues of racial justice, she had to keep her eyes and mind open—to stay vigilant and keep thinking: *I wonder if I understand this correctly.* That day with Darius, we think she did.

## Principle 3 **TAKEAWAYS**

- If you haven't experienced the headwind of bias, you'll tend to lack important knowledge about that form of bias. To address your gap in knowledge, conduct research. Before asking members of affected groups to educate you, consider whether the person wants to educate you, whether you have a close enough relationship with them, and whether the questions are not too intrusive. Even then, be careful.

- Identity conversations regularly involve "unknown unknowns," where you aren't aware of your ignorance. Adopt a learning posture by listening generously to the other person's perspective and sharing your own perspective tentatively, such as by using "I" statements and speaking in drafts.

- You might unfairly dismiss the testimony of people affected by bias. Interrupt the "running commentary of skepticism" by questioning your gut reaction when you're inclined to deny the other person's perspective. Adopt a working hypothesis that it's you who doesn't understand, not the other way around. Consider how you'd react if someone from a more privileged group told you the same story.

# Principle 4:

## **Disagree Respectfully**

On a crisp spring day in 2019, we hosted a lunchtime panel discussion in a crowded room overlooking Washington Square Park. The event brought together a group of students and administrators to share strategies for engaging in effective allyship at our law school and beyond. As we left the building and walked back to our offices, Blaine, a white male student, ran up to us on the street: "Can I ask you something?" Blaine had been silent during the event's Q&A, but he had a burning question he wanted to pose privately. "What if I say something," Blaine asked earnestly, "and a woman says it was sexist, but I don't think it was. Am I allowed to disagree?"

Discussing his question later, we agreed that moments like this one made us feel warmly toward Blaine. He'd grown up in a relatively homogeneous community and, by his own account, had thought little about social justice until he took a course at his college on the history of race. Now he'd arrived at a law school in one of the most diverse cities in the world, surrounded by students who threw around terms like "microaggressions" and "heteronormativity." The culture shock was real.

As a result of passionate identity conversations, Blaine had changed his mind on many issues. "Most of my friends back home think about racism in individual terms—how they treat the Mexican shopkeeper at the corner store. I now realize it's deeper than that." He'd become one of the more engaged straight white men on diversity and inclusion issues at the law school. Yet his views remained a few degrees off from the most progressive activists on campus.

Because we valued Blaine's freethinking spirit, our immediate response was easy to give: "Of course you're allowed to disagree!" But we knew we owed him a deeper answer. As Blaine had intuited, conversations about identity can get especially turbulent at this point. It's relatively easy to be an ally when you and the other person agree. When you disagree, you're likely to be flooded with angst and self-doubt. You might wonder: *Am I as enlightened as I thought I was? Will people feel hurt or betrayed by me?* We wanted Blaine to be able to disagree, but we also wanted to give him strategies to do it without causing unnecessary harm to himself and others. We want to offer you those strategies too.

As a starting point, we hope Principle 2 (Build Resilience) and Principle 3 (Cultivate Curiosity) will dissolve many disagreements in your life. After processing your negative emotions with resilience, you might realize you misunderstood the other person. Perhaps you thought they were calling you a misogynist, but by right-sizing their feedback you realize they were suggesting what you said revealed unconscious gender bias. After cultivating curiosity, you might conclude you were in the wrong. Maybe your comment *was* sexist, but you didn't understand the gender dimensions of the issue until you adopted a learning posture and listened generously to the other person's perspective. Don't underestimate the number of apparent disagreements that can be resolved with these potent skills.

At times, though, no amount of resilience or curiosity will be enough, and you'll be stuck with a disagreement. Here are some examples we've encountered in our work:

1. A parent thinks their children's school has leaned too far into antiracist education at the expense of more traditional aspects of the curriculum, like math or science.

2. A homeowner disagrees with their neighbor who thinks the city should take down statues of people from the past who held reprehensible views.

3. An employee thinks her manager overlooked her for a promotion because of gender bias, but he thinks he made the decision on merit.

4. A student believes universities have contributed to a growing class divide by focusing too much on racial and ethnic diversity at the expense of socioeconomic diversity.

5. Friends disagree over whether it's appropriate for an organization to fire someone for transphobic comments made over a decade ago.

When we find ourselves in disagreements like these, we sometimes pass over them in silence, and we don't beat ourselves up for that choice. Again, we contrast reflexive and reflective behaviors. We see a world of difference between staying silent because we lack the resilience and curiosity to engage, and making a calm and informed decision not to stoke unnecessary conflict.

At other times, however, we feel compelled to air the disagreement, and we suspect you'll feel the same way in many identity conversations. Without the ability to share disagreements, you'll compromise your dignity and authenticity. Your ability to demonstrate sustained allyship will also take a hit, because you won't enter many conversations about identity in the first place if you think your only option is to capitulate to whatever the other person says. Learning to disagree respectfully is a gift you give yourself, but it's also one you give to your conversation partner.

## Locate the Conversation on the Controversy Scale

We're both in same-sex relationships—Kenji married his husband in 2009, and David married his in 2014. When marriage equality was hotly debated in our home countries (the United States and Australia), we had a personal stake in the outcome. We'd both grown up feeling the bite of homophobia, and we believed bans on same-sex marriage compounded the stigma of being gay.

We participated in debates over same-sex marriage in many forums. We never enjoyed these discussions, but found one feature of them uniquely awful: our opponents rarely acknowledged what the debate meant to us, or to other LGBTQ+ people. In a prominent work opposing marriage equality, the authors insisted people could reject same-sex marriage "without denigrating same-sex-attracted people, or ignoring their needs." They took the same position in live conversations. In a televised debate about same-sex marriage with lesbian financial advisor Suze Orman, the moderator asked one of the authors, Ryan Anderson, to explain to Orman "what's wrong with her." "I don't think there's anything wrong with you," Anderson said. "The question is: What is marriage? I think that marriage is intrinsically . . . a union of a man and a woman."

Although it sounded diplomatic, this response didn't recognize that from many gay people's perspectives, Anderson's opposition to same-sex marriage logically meant he thought Orman was a second-class citizen. Many gay people understand that opponents of same-sex marriage often come from faith traditions that view homosexuality as immoral. Yet in our myriad conversations on this topic, we can count on one hand the times the opposing side recognized we might experience their view as a strike at our basic humanity. That approach wouldn't have required them to change their opinion. It would just have required them to acknowledge how that opinion might land on the other side.

In part due to that frustration, we developed a "controversy scale" that plots subjects of disagreement along a straight line. On the left are the safest subjects, where disagreement is expected or even celebrated. On the right are the most controversial subjects where the conversation is most likely to turn ugly:

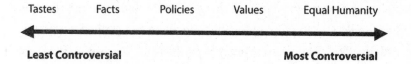

| Tastes | Facts | Policies | Values | Equal Humanity |

**Least Controversial**        **Most Controversial**

Disagreements over personal tastes are usually warm and good-natured. When friends mock us for our love of trashy TV shows, those disagreements can strengthen rather than weaken the relationship. Disagreeing over facts is also relatively comfortable, provided it really is a debate about facts (such as who, what, when, where, and how) rather than a thinly veiled debate over values (such as the vitriolic debates over "alternative facts" or "fake news"). The real danger comes when the topic drifts further to the right on the controversy scale. The most intense conversations are those where one or both sides feel their equal humanity has been put into question.

Imagine you're a Latino proponent of an affirmative action program, and you're debating a non-Latino colleague who opposes the program. We think you'll find it uncomfortable but manageable to discuss whether affirmative action has reduced ethnic inequality in your school (facts). You'll find it harder to debate whether access to college education should be based only on supposedly objective criteria like test scores (values). And you'll find it excruciating to debate psychologist Richard Herrnstein and political scientist Charles Murray's infamous hypothesis that IQs differ among racial and ethnic groups (equal humanity).

The trouble with identity disagreements is that more privileged people and less privileged people almost always locate the issue at different positions on the controversy scale. If you think your children's school focuses too much on antiracist education, you may see the dispute as a policy debate over the appropriate balance among different parts of the curriculum. Your conversation partner, an Asian American mother, may think you're trivializing her child's sense of belonging at the school. She's the one, after all, who has to comfort her son when he's bullied with comments like "Go back to where you came from." You locate the issue in the middle of the controversy scale at "policies." She locates it at the rightward extreme of "equal humanity."

You may find that when you empathize with the other person's situation, you'll reassess the nature of the disagreement, moving the issue closer to where they've placed it on the scale. But you might not, and we're not pushing you to do so. All we ask is that you explicitly acknowledge your counterpart's position. At the outset of the conversation, you might say something like: "To me this is a policy debate, but I see how it could be deeply personal for you, and I'll do my best to respect that reality when sharing my views." There might also be times during or after a conversation where you realize you treated the topic as a purely intellectual exercise and need to recognize the impact the discussion might have had on the other person: "I've been bringing policy arguments to the table, but can I ask how you've been experiencing this discussion as someone whose life may be more directly affected by this issue?" Routinely, allies fail to take these simple but critical steps.

## Find Uncommon Commonalities

In the movie *Predator*, the character of Dutch (played by Arnold Schwarzenegger) and the character of Dillon (played by Carl Weathers) greet each other with what's come to be known as an "epic handshake." "Dillon, you son of a bitch," Dutch says as they walk up to each other and clasp their hands together with their hulking arms in a V-shape like they're about to arm-wrestle. They refuse to let go of each other's hand. Then the handshake turns into an actual arm-wrestling match. It's an almost parodic display of over-the-top masculinity.

The scene might have been forgotten but for a viral meme. When social media users want to show two people, two groups, or two concepts that seem unrelated but share a surprising commonality, they post a picture of Dutch and Dillon shaking hands. They put one label over Dutch's arm, another over Dillon's arm, and the commonality in the middle. In one instance, revenge and ice cream shake hands over the phrase "best served cold." In another, influencers and construction workers unite over "Carhartt beanies." The epic handshake has also spawned other attempts at highlighting unpredictable overlaps using Venn diagrams. We learn, for instance, that bank robbers, DJs, and preachers share "put your hands up." Therapists, four-year-olds, and the Backstreet Boys all say "tell me why." These images help us see the commonalities in every conflict, the handshake hidden in each arm-wrestling match.

This capability is critical, and harder than it looks to cultivate. It's conventional wisdom that offering points of agreement is an effective strategy when disagreeing with someone. But as philosopher Daniel Dennett notes, it's particularly helpful to find points that "are not matters of general or widespread agreement." The idea is to find uncommon commonalities that surprise you out of your defaults. Too often, people settle for the bland ones that feel like empty gestures. They do the equivalent of posting the bank robbers, DJs, and preachers meme, but making the commonality "occupations."

Consider a topic of disagreement that's ubiquitous on social media, in classrooms, and at a barbecue or water cooler near you: cancel culture. Many people take issue with the tendency to ostracize and shame people who make mistakes on identity issues. In a memorable example, over 150 public figures, including Margaret Atwood, Steven Pinker, and Gloria Steinem, shared their objections to cancel culture in an open letter in *Harper's Magazine* soon after the historic uprisings for racial justice in 2020. The letter's signatories slammed the climate of "blinding moral certainty" and "censoriousness" on identity issues, which they claimed was threatening "the lifeblood of a liberal society." Given the timing of the letter, the authors understandably tried to acknowledge common ground with their opponents. "Powerful protests for racial and social justice are leading to overdue demands for police reform, along with wider calls for greater equality and inclusion across our society, not least in higher education, journalism, philanthropy, and the arts," the letter started. "But," it continued, "this needed reckoning has also intensified a new set of moral attitudes and political commitments that tend to weaken our norms of open debate and toleration of differences in favor of ideological conformity." The balance of the letter recited a host of reasons why claims for equality and inclusion had led to "dogma," "coercion," "intolerance," a "stifling atmosphere," and "public shaming and ostracism."

We deeply respect many of the signatories of this letter, and understand that it's hard to align on language when so many authors are involved. We also agree with their conclusion that it's time to hit the pause button on cancel culture. But we think the letter still fell short in its attempt at finding commonalities. By applauding "calls for greater equality and inclusion across our society," it found a commonality that was broad to the point of sounding vapid. The letter also turned so quickly to the long list of disagreements that it made the earlier point of agreement seem like throat-clearing.

Finding uncommon commonalities will often liberate you as well as your conversation partner. We can draw an analogy here with feelings. In the influential book *Difficult Conversations*, the authors point out that intense emotions can be consuming—if you're angry at your sibling, the anger tends to obliterate everything else. Yet this experience is a distortion—you'll usually have other emotions about your sibling, including positive ones. It's both more honest and more productive to give a full and nuanced description: "It's because I love you that this recent incident hurt and angered me." Similarly, in disagreements, you're likely to fixate too much on the points of contention because they're the sources of pain. If you can add in all the ways you're in sync with the other person, you'll find the band of agreement wider and richer than you thought. Finding common ground will jolt you out of your relentless focus on where you differ and give you a more panoramic view.

As you look for commonalities, be sure to credit your conversation partner for their contributions. Behavioral scientist Xuan Zhao and her colleagues have found that responding to another person's point of view with the statement "Thank you, because . . ." builds common ground far more effectively than shopworn expressions like "I hear that." The words "Thank you, because . . ." (or equivalents like "I appreciate you sharing that perspective; I hadn't thought of it that way") signal not only that you acknowledge the other person's point of view, but also that you value it. These statements lead your conversation partner to feel more heard and respected and to perceive the exchange as more collaborative. Other research shows that simply pledging to take the other person's perspective seriously and to discuss it equally alongside yours can defuse an otherwise contentious political argument.

Dave Isay, a radio producer, created an initiative called "One Small Step" that brings strangers together to talk face-to-face for fifty minutes. The program matches people who disagree about politics but have something else in common. At the outset, the facilitators ask the participants to read their biographies out loud. In a conversation featured on *60 Minutes*, participant Brenda Brown-Grooms opens: "I grew up as an army brat and evangelical Christian surrounded by a very powerful ideology of conservatism, patriotism, and religion." Her interlocutor, Nicole Unice, responds: "I am a Baptist pastor and performance artist, a native Charlottesvillian, graduate of the University of Virginia and Union Theological Seminary in New York City." Immediately they see the overlap. "We're pastors," says Brown-Grooms, "and we're helping people to find their path and find their voice." Unice agrees: "Oh, Brenda, I love what you just said about helping people find their path, because I feel such a connection there."

This strategy of finding uncommon commonalities can help

make even the most inflammatory of subjects easier to discuss. In recent years, hordes of concerned parents have streamed into usually sleepy town hall meetings to express outrage over the conversations about race being held in their children's classrooms. One such parent is Bart Glasgow (no relation to David), a conservative evangelical Christian white man from Canton, Georgia, who spoke up at a school board meeting to oppose the hiring of a diversity, equity, and inclusion administrator in his local district.

Bart and his wife, Coley, decided to speak with four experts on the subject of race. One was Carol Anderson, a professor and chair of African American studies at Emory University and author of books like *White Rage*. On the surface, Anderson and the Glasgows have little in common. Yet in their hour-long conversation, both sides made considerable effort to find points of connection. Bart Glasgow noted that he wrote his senior college thesis on the topic of civil disobedience, examining figures like Henry David Thoreau, Mahatma Gandhi, and Martin Luther King Jr. "I think what Dr. King did was amazing," he said. "To take that biblical principle of turning the other cheek and to show love when hate's being shown to you." Anderson noted her father was "career military" and described being raised in the church and in a "God-fearing" community. They all bonded over their experience growing up with the *World Book Encyclopedia* in their homes and with parents who would take them "to the woodshed." They continued by sharing experiences of being in the minority in an educational setting. Anderson talked about being bussed to a majority-white high school. Coley Glasgow, who is white, shared that she completed her higher education at two historically black colleges.

This exploration of common ground paid dividends. As the conversation continued, they aired disagreements. Bart Glasgow argued against an emphasis on systemic racism: "If something is systemic, there's a tendency to say, 'No one's to blame.' . . . To me it undercuts personal accountability." Anderson disagreed: "It's not one or the other. We have to recognize the system that we're in that creates these hierarchies. . . . We also have to recognize the role of personal responsibility and making good choices." Later, Bart advocated for school vouchers that would allow parents to move their children out of underperforming local schools. Anderson responded that "vouchers have not proven to be the answer" and argued that public schools needed more resources. Bart said that when he looked at the budgets of local school districts online, he concluded that "it's obviously not a funding issue." He pressed Anderson again on school vouchers. Anderson stood her ground: "I am not a fan of vouchers." Yet these disagreements were remarkably civil. When the conversation came to a close, Bart said to Anderson: "I could talk to you for hours. I really could." Anderson replied: "Thank you so much for being here and asking these wonderful questions and engaging in this great conversation. Thank you. I love it."

## Show Your Work

Shortly after we launched our research center, we received an unnerving email from a respected colleague. She asked us to use our platform as diversity and inclusion scholars to advocate for people who don't fully vaccinate themselves or their children. In her view, excluding people from schools and workplaces for defying vaccine mandates had "troubling" implications for the values of diversity, inclusion, and belonging. She invited us to discuss the issue with her so it could be addressed university-wide.

We received this request before the COVID-19 pandemic turned vaccines into a white-hot issue. Even so, we knew this conversation might be difficult. We passionately disagreed with her perspective. And we feared no amount of acknowledging her position on the controversy scale or epic handshakes would suffice.

So we shared our reasoning in depth. We stated politely but firmly that we didn't believe opposition to vaccines fit within the scope of our center's work. We explained that the center's primary function was to address bias against marginalized social groups, like people of color or women. We acknowledged that some groups like religious minorities were mistreated because of their beliefs rather than because of their physical characteristics. But particularly as a newly launched center, we weren't eager to stretch the definition of a marginalized group to people defined by their views on a single issue. We also noted that the topic of vaccine hesitancy raised complicated medical, ethical, and public health questions outside our expertise.

We had no illusions that this approach would change our colleague's mind. But it showed we'd given her viewpoint real consideration and it also offered her an opportunity to point out where we might be wrong. She thanked us for our "thoughtful" response, noted she completely understood our position, and invited us to participate in an event on a separate topic.

Our approach to our colleague's inquiry was an example of "showing your work"—sharing a disagreement in as much detail as possible to demonstrate to the other person that you've thought carefully about the subject. The advice to highlight points of disagreement may seem out of step with our previous emphasis on finding common ground. But you can and should do both—look for points of agreement *and* share points of disagreement in detail. Paint a complete picture of the facts and values on which you're basing your disagreement, any research and conversations that have informed your current thinking, and any remaining doubts or uncertainties you hold. Over your conversation partner's lifetime, they've probably encountered many people who have reflexively opposed their views based on shoddy or incomplete work. Showing the effort you've made will distinguish you from those opponents. It will help them respond to you rather than to all those voices from their past.

A word of caution: when showing your work, don't offer a slapdash summary of the opposing argument before immediately dismissing it. Writer Moira Weigel has likened this mistake to "the first sentence of the last paragraph" of a high-school essay: "I have thought of the other side already. Do not accuse me of not having thought of the other side!" Rather than taking that cursory approach, take the time to research and understand the opposing view, and then share that understanding generously before you explain why you continue to see the issue differently. Show your work to show your respect.

## Manage Your Expectations

Many people have a low tolerance for disagreement in general. If a contentious identity issue comes up at the dinner table, they immediately change the subject or take a giant swig of wine. If they have an argument with someone, they replay the conversation in their mind for weeks. David, unfortunately, is one such person. He'll run away from voicing a disagreement to avoid conflict, then stew alone in frustration that the other person doesn't agree with him. For whatever reason, he seems to have an unrealistic expectation that identity conversations should always end in a group hug.

People sometimes ask us anguished questions that come from a similar place, like: "I'm an atheist and staunch liberal but a colleague on my team at work is a conservative evangelical Christian. How can we work together despite our disagreements?" Our answer: lower your expectations. We admit this advice probably won't make its way onto a motivational poster. But we think it's completely appropriate to scale the intensity of the passion you bring into the disagreement to the intensity of the relationship.

A comic by Randall Munroe shows a stick figure furiously tapping away at a computer keyboard. A voice from the other room calls out: "Are you coming to bed?" The stick figure responds: "I can't. This is important. Someone is *wrong* on the internet." Most people have enough perspective not to care fiercely about disagreements with random internet trolls. But it's worth cultivating that healthy instinct in other situations too. Both of us would struggle if we had major disagreements with our spouses about issues of identity. Nevertheless, we've both supervised and advanced the careers of students who disagree with us, because the teacher-student relationship is less intense than the marital one. The same goes for colleagues, neighbors, and acquaintances. When the relationship isn't as close, the need for agreement should be lower.

You can also manage your expectations of what can be achieved in a single conversation. As with any dispute on a heavy subject, identity conflicts often aren't neatly resolved in one encounter. The first conversation might go poorly, but the second might go better and the third better still. You might need to take multiple off-ramps and on-ramps to and from a conversation before you make progress.

## Why the Four Strategies Can Fail

Even with the benefit of these four strategies, you might think we're being unrealistic about your ability to disagree agreeably on matters of identity. A common complaint we hear especially from people with moderate or conservative viewpoints is that "you're not allowed to disagree anymore." Employee surveys we've conducted inside organizations have surfaced comments like "I must endure all types of viewpoints that advocate for social and political 'progress' but can't present my own viewpoint without putting my job at risk."

To explain why our strategies sometimes fail despite your best efforts, we need to start with the insight that not all disagreements are created equal. Think about how you react to the following three disagreements about gender.

The first example is from our teaching. In our courses, we sometimes discuss "gender quotas"—policies that fix a minimum percentage of women in government or corporate leadership positions. Quotas are a well-established practice in many countries, but the topic always sparks spirited debate in our class. Some students believe quotas are necessary to achieve gender equality in a reasonable time frame. Others argue quotas aren't merit-based, or that they harm women by giving the appearance their positions are unearned.

The second example comes from the prominent white nationalist Richard Spencer, who questioned whether women should be allowed to vote. His comment echoed a similar remark he made about women's fitness for public office. Referring to Hillary Clinton, he argued: "Women should never be allowed to make foreign policy. It's not that they're 'weak.' To the contrary, their vindictiveness knows no bounds."

The third disagreement comes from Google engineer James Damore, who circulated a ten-page memo to his colleagues criticizing many of the company's gender equity efforts. According to Damore, innate biological differences "may explain why we don't see equal representation of women in tech and leadership." The memo called for an "open and honest discussion about the costs and benefits of our diversity programs."

When we share examples like these, most people have a clear intuition that the first one is a legitimate disagreement. Sure, they might have a strong view for or against gender quotas, but they can usually tolerate differences of opinion without thinking their opponents are malicious or chauvinistic. In stark contrast, people usually find the second example clearly illegitimate. In our society today, decent people don't "respectfully disagree" over whether women should retain the right to vote or be allowed to serve in government, and it's offensive even to entertain the argument. The third one creates the most division. In our own social and professional circles, many people find Damore's position illegitimate even to entertain, much like Spencer's. But if you step outside our bubble, it's not hard to find people who think it's legitimate to debate whether innate gender differences influence choices about careers and areas of study. As with the topic of gender quotas, those individuals may have strong opinions on the substance of Damore's argument, but they think it is, or should be, socially acceptable to disagree.

The point here is that disagreements don't just happen at an individual level. They also happen in a social context. When we're analyzing disagreements at a societal level, we like to use traffic-light coding. We call disagreements "green" when most people in a given society at a given time believe it's acceptable to disagree on that issue. By contrast, we call identity disagreements "red" when society long ago achieved consensus on a topic, and the vast majority of people believe it's wrong to rehash the disagreement now. Finally, we call an identity disagreement "yellow" when large swaths of people across a society split over whether a disagreement is acceptable or unacceptable.

Yellow disagreements are in many ways the hardest of all. They usually occur when norms are changing—when social movements have challenged old ways of thinking but haven't fully replaced them. In yellow situations, some people think the issue has been debated enough and it's time for society to move on and treat it as red. Others say no, society should keep discussing the issue and it's unfair to try to shut down debate.

To be clear, when we label disagreements as green, red, or yellow, we're not making a personal assessment about whether they're legitimate or illegitimate. Rather, we're describing what the population of a society happens to think at a specific point in time. In our view, denying women the right to vote has always been morally abhorrent—it should have been obvious in all times and places that women are equal to men. Yet the debate on this topic was a green one in our society and many comparable societies in the late nineteenth and early twentieth centuries. Similarly, the topic of gender quotas is green today, but it's possible that a century from now most people will look back aghast that anyone could ever have opposed them, which would make a debate on that subject red.

A topic can sometimes shift from one category to another at a disorienting speed, as illustrated by the marriage equality debate. As we noted, we found debates over same-sex marriage grueling at an individual level when we had them in the 2000s and the early 2010s. Nonetheless, when we panned out to a societal level, we recognized the topic was a green disagreement at that time. Our societies were working through a significant evolution in their understanding of gay rights and the meaning of marriage. Yet if someone tried to reopen the marriage equality debate in our society today, we'd find it harder to entertain the disagreement.

So if you try to voice a disagreement using our strategies and it still goes terribly, ask yourself: Is this a yellow topic? You may think you're unlikely to be in that position, but we know from experience that even people who are allies of social justice in a broad sense can disagree on a yellow issue from time to time. Given the rapid pace of change in society, it's possible your (or our) views on some topics will be seen as outdated or prejudiced in the years ahead.

When you're in a yellow disagreement, we recommend you exercise greater caution. The traffic-light analogy offers guidance here. For red disagreements, our advice is to stop to avoid a multi-car pileup. For green disagreements you can go ahead and drive, but you still need to exercise ordinary caution by steering, signaling, and the like. The four strategies we've outlined can be viewed as the rules of the road. Yellow disagreements are in the middle. When you see a yellow light, you should obey the same road rules, but you should also feel less confident you can successfully "make the light." The yellow light signals you need to make a more careful set of additional judgments before moving forward, not least because the light could change to red.

What might that extra caution look like? You could start by doing more research before sharing your opinion. After reading more and listening with greater curiosity to the people most affected by the issue, you may be persuaded that your initial viewpoint was incorrect. If you continue to disagree, you might consider hashing out your viewpoint with someone who doesn't belong to the affected group but who holds a different position from you. Finally, if you decide to share your opinion with someone from the affected community, our best advice is to follow our four strategies, while managing your expectations even more resolutely than you normally would. Don't be surprised if the other person finds it impossible to engage in a "respectful" dialogue on a yellow disagreement when they find the entire debate fundamentally disrespectful.

꘎

We said we owed our student Blaine a deeper answer than "Of course you're allowed to disagree!" Now we can offer it to him and to you.

In a free society, we think it's essential that people have the ability to air disagreements on issues of identity, diversity, and justice. We also think such freedom comes with a moral responsibility to speak with care. Many people pit the values of inclusion and free speech against each other, as though we must all choose between completely censoring ourselves and thoughtlessly offending others. In her book *Dare to Speak*, human rights advocate Suzanne Nossel resoundingly rejects that false choice. She argues that inclusion and free speech are, in fact, complementary values. In her view, speaking "conscientiously," such as by avoiding stereotypes and other demeaning language, "can enable everyone to speak more freely." We agree. A culture of free speech can and should go hand in hand with a culture of respect.

People who haven't learned to disagree conscientiously tend to view these conversations solely in terms of damage control. Now that you have this skill, we think you can find a higher purpose. Few if any meaningful relationships are devoid of conflict. When handled well, moments of tension can deepen a bond. Rather than nodding along insincerely or offering fake opinions, sharing a thoughtful difference of opinion can show the other person you value them enough to be honest with them.

Sometimes, of course, the rift between you and the other person will be too wide. Sometimes an attempt at conversation will end without a resolution. Sometimes the relationship itself will end. As awful as that outcome can feel, it's sometimes a necessary one. We're not here to guarantee that every disagreement will end happily. Rather, we want to help you ensure that a divide is truly unbridgeable before you walk away from it.

When relationships are damaged through no fault of either party, that outcome is painful enough. Unfortunately, in identity conversations, many rifts do have a culprit. If we could, we'd make sure you could dodge the four conversational traps and engage in these dialogues with exquisite emotional and intellectual maturity at all times. Alas, we are human, and so are you. You'll inevitably say the wrong thing in some of these conversations and hurt someone you care about. In such situations, you need a new skill. It's time to learn the art of the apology.

## Principle 4 **TAKEAWAYS**

- Locate the conversation on the "controversy scale." To you the conversation may be a factual or policy debate, but to the other person it may be a debate over their equal humanity.

- Find uncommon commonalities—points of agreement that are not matters of widespread agreement—and thank the other person when they make valuable contributions to the conversation.

- Show your work on remaining disagreements to demonstrate you've thought carefully about the subject.

- Manage your expectations. Scale the intensity with which you care about the disagreement to the intensity of the relationship.

- Recognize that at a societal level, identity disagreements come in three forms: "green" disagreements, where most people in a society think it's acceptable to disagree on the issue; "red" disagreements, where people overwhelmingly think the disagreement is unacceptable; and "yellow" disagreements, where large swaths of people vehemently contest whether the disagreement is acceptable or unacceptable.

- For yellow disagreements, exercise greater caution. Conduct more research before sharing your opinion, consider hashing out your views with people outside of the affected group, and manage your expectations even more resolutely.

# Principle 5:

## **Apologize Authentically**

In a book titled *The Apology*, a man apologizes to his adult daughter for abusing her as a child. The man's apology describes his horrific acts of physical and emotional violence, as well as his attempts at victim-blaming his daughter: "I worked daily to destroy your character and break your will. . . . I made you believe things about yourself that were never true." The apology unflinchingly details the wrongs he committed and the impact of his behavior. "No longer carefree, chatty, and inquisitive, you became depressed and withdrawn," the man recalls. "You moved like a ghost. You rarely lifted your head and hardly spoke. You never washed your hair and it was always stringy and dirty. You were unable to concentrate in school and did poorly in class."

The man takes full responsibility for the harm he inflicted: "Was I a psychopath? That would be an easy out. No. I was not insane. I was a privileged, forceful man." "I betrayed your trust," he continues. "You did not and could not give me permission. There was no consent." His remorse is fervent: "I am filled with horror and regret, feeling for the first time how you must have felt." He concludes: "Let me say these words: I am sorry. I am sorry."

This striking apology has a crucial flaw: it's fake. The book was written by the author known as V (formerly Eve Ensler), the survivor of the abuse. The perpetrator, her father, is dead. Reeling from an abusive childhood, V waited decades for an apology that never came. In a TED talk delivered at the beginning of the #MeToo movement, she noted: "I have never heard a man who has committed rape or physical violence ever publicly apologize to his victim." This culture of non-apology led her to wonder: "What would an authentic, deep apology be like?" Her book came as the answer to that question: "I began to write, and my father's voice began to come through me."

V's observation that male abusers don't apologize calls attention to a much wider problem. People with privilege often have a hard time apologizing for a variety of harms, even those falling well short of physical abuse. Psychiatrist Aaron Lazare points out that members of dominant groups disproportionately adopt a "never regret, never explain, never apologize" attitude. Channeling her father's voice, V writes: "I don't remember ever apologizing for anything. In fact, it was drilled into me that to apologize was to expose weakness." Growing up, we both remember hearing that message directed at men, and we work hard today to ignore its destructive call.

We assume you, like us, reject the uncompromising position of "never apologize." You can resist the urge to defend yourself reflexively. You know how to listen to other people's perspectives with resilience and curiosity. Your difficulty is not in realizing you owe an apology. It's in finding the words to express it.

That struggle is understandable, because few have been trained in how to apologize. "When a child hurts someone else, say, another child, the conventional practice is to teach the child to mumble a rote, pro forma 'I'm sorry,' as if that's what is needed," psychologist Molly Howes observes. "Children learn to say words they don't understand and therefore don't mean." Even after studying apologies, we regularly fall into this trap with our own children. It's so much easier to extract the buzzwords "I'm sorry" from them than to slow down and make sure they've done the subtler and more painstaking work of healing the harm.

We sense another explanation for why apologies are hard that continues into adulthood. Apologies make you acutely vulnerable. What if you admit error and your conversation partner takes the opportunity to pile on? What if your apology exposes you to public shaming or a lawsuit? What if you're forced to see something about yourself you didn't want to see?

If you know you should apologize but have these qualms, it's natural to split the difference. You might hedge or add conditions to your apologies—"I'm sorry if," "I'm sorry but"—to signal your contrition while limiting your exposure. Such qualifications are often unconscious. Yet by trying to have it both ways, you usually succeed at neither objective. The recipient thinks you're not sincerely sorry, and your ambivalent apology makes you more, not less, vulnerable to criticism.

We think it's worth soldiering through these difficulties, because if you can offer an authentic apology, you can do wonders for yourself and the other person. As psychologist Harriet Lerner says, "'I'm sorry' are the two most healing words in the English language." Others have noted the almost mystical effect of apologies. Consultant John Kador calls the apology "humanity's perfect response to imperfection." "In some cases," he observes, "the relationship is actually stronger for having been broken and reconciled."

To give an effective apology, you need to satisfy the "four Rs" of recognition, responsibility, remorse, and redress. Giving an authentic apology isn't like completing a checklist, so you can't work through these elements mechanically. The four Rs can, however, serve as useful guideposts to ensure you're on the right path.

## Recognition (No Ifpologies)

Comedian and television host Ellen DeGeneres had made "be kind" her motto. Yet in a series of bombshell *BuzzFeed* reports, current and former employees characterized her iconic talk show as a toxic workplace, alleging everything from racism to sexual harassment. "That 'be kind' bullshit only happens when the cameras are on," one former employee fumed.

When the show returned the next season, DeGeneres addressed the allegations—vaguely. "I learned that things happened here that never should have happened," she observed without specifying the "things." She then said curtly that the show had "made the necessary changes" and that she was "starting a new chapter." Later in the monologue, she added: "If I've ever let someone down, if I've ever hurt their feelings, I am so sorry for that. If that's ever the case, I have let myself down and I've hurt myself as well." One outlet panned DeGeneres's words by noting that her "strange apology won't satisfy anybody," while another hyperbolically suggested it might be "the worst apology of all time."

DeGeneres's apology is an example of what comedian Harry Shearer has dubbed an "ifpology." By repeating the word "if," she made the harm sound uncertain. Yet if she was genuinely uncertain about the harm, she should have asked more questions before flicking over the page. Her failure to do that left the apology in limbo. "The liberation is in the details," V says. "An apology is a remembering. It connects the past with the present. It says that what occurred actually did occur." However well meant, formulations like "if I've ever let someone down" acknowledge nothing.

Another variety of ifpology questions the recipient's reaction to the wrong, rather than the wrong itself—"I'm sorry if you take it that way" or "I'm sorry if you're offended." At their worst, these apologies seek to shift the blame, effectively saying: "I'm sorry if you're so tightly wound that you can't see your reaction is overblown." Yet even in the most generous interpretation, where the apologizer is genuinely uncertain about the harm, these ifpologies could still benefit from more curiosity. Again, if you're unsure whether someone is offended, why not ask?

We saw a vivid example of such an ifpology when a young woman, Miya Ponsetto, physically accosted a fourteen-year-old Black boy in a hotel lobby because she wrongly believed he'd stolen her phone. In a TV interview, Ponsetto addressed the boy's family: "I do sincerely from the bottom of my heart apologize . . . if I made the son feel as if I assaulted him or if I hurt his feelings." Ponsetto said the following year that she wished she'd "apologized differently." Nonetheless, "if I made the son feel as if I assaulted him" was an outlandish way of putting it. Security footage showed Ponsetto tackling the boy as he walked across the lobby.

Don't ascribe too much magic to the word "if," because any qualifying language can have the same effect. Consider a request for blanket immunity: "Whatever I did, I'm sorry." We've both received apologies like this, and they failed because they were too general, as if the person couldn't be bothered to explore or acknowledge what they'd done.

Another instance of an ifpology without the "if" occurred when Harriet Lerner was talking with other parents about the lack of diversity at her children's school. A fellow parent said her son had two Black children in his class, "but they seem clean and well behaved." Another parent challenged the comment: "Black but clean and well behaved? Help me understand what you mean here." The woman became flustered. The next day, she approached the father who had challenged her: "I'm really sorry you heard my comment as racist." Like Lerner, we admire his dignified response: "If you see the problem as my reaction, and not what you said, I'm afraid I can't accept your apology."

Just as nonrecognition can dispirit, true recognition can inspire. The children's film *The Witches*, based on the Roald Dahl book of the same name, depicts villainous witches with split hands and feet. This portrayal outraged many in the disability community, as the witches looked like they had ectrodactyly, a condition where one or more digits from the hands or feet are absent. Anne Hathaway, who played the Grand High Witch in the film, apologized: "I am sorry. I did not connect limb difference with the GHW when the look of the character was brought to me; if I had, I assure you this never would have happened." She continued: "I particularly want to say I'm sorry to kids with limb differences: now that I know better I promise I'll do better. And I owe a special apology to everyone who loves you as fiercely as I love my own kids: I'm sorry I let your family down." To this apology, she attached a video on the topic of limb difference from a disability advocacy organization. What we admire most about Hathaway's apology is that she took an unblinking look at the harm and educated herself, which in turn allowed her to educate others.

## Responsibility (No Butpologies)

In the early hours of the morning, comedian Roseanne Barr posted a tweet that would catapult her into that day's news headlines.

She wrote that if the Muslim Brotherhood and the Planet of the Apes "had a baby," it would be Valerie Jarrett, a Black senior White House advisor. The reaction was immediate and scorching. Barr's costar Sara Gilbert tweeted that Barr's comments were "abhorrent." In a literal cancellation, ABC pulled the plug on her hit show, *Roseanne.*

As the controversy swirled around her, Barr wrote a flurry of tweets, including an apology. At one point, she acknowledged she had "made a mistake," calling the original tweet "egregious" and "indefensible." Yet in the same statement, Barr noted: "It was 2 in the morning and I was Ambien tweeting." This bizarre observation led the manufacturer of the sleeping pill Ambien to clarify that "racism is not a known side effect of any Sanofi medication."

Barr's failed apology was a "butpology," because it acknowledged the harm while denying responsibility for it. As in Barr's case, butpologies often excuse bad behavior based on circumstances in the person's life: "I'm sorry, but I was having a miserable day," or "I'm sorry, but I was stressed." When you make appeals like these, you not only seek to duck responsibility, but you also suggest the harm could recur. If you say, "I'm sorry, but I was having a miserable day," your conversation partner could fairly wonder if you'll repeat your behavior when you have another one.

Even in her weird medical explanation, Barr isn't alone. Many people have offered this form of butpology for racial slurs, as if they find it so unbearable to have crossed that line that they need a note from their doctor. Michelle Odinet, a judge in Louisiana, was caught on video using the n-word while watching security footage of an attempted burglary at her home. "I am deeply sorry and ask for your forgiveness and understanding," she said in a written statement. She also included the disclaimer: "I was given a sedative at the time of the video. I have zero recollection of the video and the disturbing language used during it." Sports announcer Matt Rowan also said the n-word on a hot mic, while chiding the players of a girls' basketball team for kneeling during the national anthem to protest racial injustice. In his apology, Rowan said: "I wholeheartedly accept responsibility for my words and actions." At the same time, he explained he had type 1 diabetes. "While not excusing my remarks," he said, "it is not unusual when my sugar spikes that I become disoriented and often say things that are not appropriate as well as hurtful."

In fairness, providing context for your actions can sometimes be helpful. Depending on how severe your behavior was, the other person might feel less of a negative impact if they learn you were going through a difficult patch and acted out of character. When you're tempted to offer an explanation, the best question is whether you're offering it for yourself or for the other person. Are you saying, "Please excuse my behavior because it wasn't the real me," or are you saying, "It *was* the real me, but not the me I aspire to be"?

Another classic form of butpology deflects to intent: "I'm sorry, but I didn't mean it." In a video on how to apologize, You-Tuber Franchesca Ramsey discusses a prior video called "Queen for a Day," in which she walked through city streets dressed as a drag queen and asked people to guess whether she was a man or a woman. When a critic called her out for posting "transphobic garbage," her immediate reaction was to jump to her intentions: "I have friends that are trans! I didn't mean it that way." But Ramsey then learned that for many trans individuals, "having someone try to figure out what your gender is" can be "a daily battle." She saw that she'd made a "game" out of an issue that had serious consequences, including physical violence, for that community. She apologized and concluded that her intentions in making the first video were irrelevant. "It doesn't matter in these instances what you meant," she said. "What matters is what's the outcome of what you said or what you did."

We first introduced the distinction between intent and impact in Principle 1 (Beware the Four Conversational Traps), where we discussed the error of deflecting to good intentions. This distinction is foundational in diversity and inclusion work. In a representative essay, consultant Jamie Utt asks rhetorically, "What does the intent of our action really matter if our actions have the impact of furthering the marginalization or oppression of those around us?"

We agree with practitioners in our field who focus on impact more than on intent. As Ramsey observed in her video, just because a person didn't intend to step on your foot doesn't mean you're not in pain. At the risk of irking our colleagues, however, we believe it goes too far to say intent is irrelevant. Even if you think impact is critical (as we do), sometimes intent can affect the impact of an action. As jurist Oliver Wendell Holmes Jr. said, "even a dog distinguishes between being stumbled over and being kicked." We suspect you'd feel worse if you knew someone stepped on your foot on purpose.

How, then, can you distinguish good references to intent from bad ones? Again, we believe everything depends on the reason you invoke it. If you use intent to diminish the consequences for yourself, we think it's unhelpful. If you offer it so the other person can properly assess the impact of your actions, we believe it can play a positive role.

High-school teacher Andrew Puckey offers an example of a helpful reference. Puckey used the phrase "All Lives Matter" at the end of a student awards ceremony. While "All Lives Matter" sounds harmless without context, people typically use this slogan to deflect from "Black Lives Matter." It's a form of upswitching, as we discussed in Principle 1 (Beware the Four Conversational Traps). Actor Arthur Chu likens saying "All Lives Matter" to crashing a stranger's funeral and shouting, "I too have felt loss!"

Puckey, however, apparently didn't realize the negative sense of the phrase. As part of a larger apology posted to the school district's website, he stated: "Over the last few days, I have been given the opportunity to review how the phrase 'All Lives Matter' has been used to discount the Black Lives Matter movement. Given the current state of affairs in our country, the use of this phrase is completely disrespectful. Although my intention was to tell students that they were important, and to show kindness to one another, these three words negated everything I said, leaving only a perception of racism and intolerance. For this, I am deeply sorry." He added that his choice of words was "inappropriate" and "caused hurt to many in our community," especially students of color, and that he was "profoundly sorry for using a phrase that is connected to prejudice." As we read Puckey's apology, he shared his intentions to soften the impact of the words, not to evade responsibility for them. Put differently, he conveyed the helpful message: "Even though my intentions were good, the impact of my words was harmful." He steered clear of its unhelpful mirror image: "Even though the impact of my words was harmful, my intentions were good."

A third form of butpology deflects to your character with statements like "I'm sorry, but I'm not a racist." This rejoinder is everywhere. Pop singer Madonna used the n-word in a hashtag on social media. Then she apologized: "I am sorry if I offended anyone with my use of the N word on Instagram. It was not meant as a racial slur. I am not a racist." English women's football coach Phil Neville apologized for sexist tweets by noting: "I had to apologize. I didn't like the words used. I'm not a sexist. I've lived my life right." David Simms, a hockey commentator, apologized for saying it was "disgusting" to show a gay male couple kissing on camera, adding: "I am not homophobic; you have known me long enough. I haven't got a bad bone in my body."

Here we have unequivocal advice: stay away from these formulations. Applying our test of whether the explanation is for you or for your conversation partner, we view statements like "I'm sorry, but I'm not a sexist" to be almost inherently self-interested. The logic seems to be: "I may have done something terrible, but I'm not a sexist in the sense of being an avowed male chauvinist." These statements sound like you're trying to exonerate yourself by saying your behavior could have been far worse.

Viewed in a more sympathetic light, the logic could be: "I may have said something sexist, but I'm not a sexist person. Please separate what I do from who I am." We fully agree a person's actions should be distinguished from their identity. As we discussed in Principle 2 (Build Resilience), moving from a fixed to a growth mindset requires that distinction. But a person in a growth mindset wouldn't say: "Give me a pass on my bad behavior because I'm a good person." Rather, they'd say: "My behavior wasn't good enough. I'll try to learn from this mistake so I can live up to my ideals."

The clearest way to see how frustrating butpologies can be is to contrast them with apologies that squarely take responsibility. Like Odinet, Rowan, and Madonna, former *Bachelorette* star Hannah Brown used the n-word—she'd been singing a rap song on Instagram Live when she blurted it out. Initially, like the others, she dodged responsibility with a hedging apology: "I really don't think I said that word. . . . And even if I did accidentally say it, I'm very sorry, I was singing a song and not even thinking." Yet she ultimately returned to give a proper apology in an extended video on Instagram. Noting she had spent the intervening time educating herself on racial issues and reflecting on her behavior, she observed: "I don't want to be ignorant anymore. . . . I have learned that I have to take a lot of responsibility and accountability for my actions." Brown then addressed her fans directly, many of whom had been rallying around her: "If you want to support me, do not defend me. What I said, what I did, was indefensible. . . . If you want to support me, then just continue to encourage me to be better and go on this journey with me. . . . What I said, what I did, was wrong."

## Remorse (No Fauxpologies)

Remorse is the crux of an apology—an acknowledgment you've caused someone pain and want to make it right. For this reason, it might seem like the simplest component of an apology. Yet here be dragons. Even the words "I'm sorry" are treacherous, because the phrase can convey condolence ("I'm sorry you're upset") rather than contrition ("I'm sorry you're upset because I mocked your religion"). One of our students always uses the phrase "I apologize" instead of "I'm sorry" to remove any doubt about what she means. We ourselves haven't discarded the word "sorry," but we appreciate her point that contrition is much harder to express than condolence. It's so easy to slip from the first to the second that it's wise to be vigilant.

We call apologies that fail to express remorse "fauxpologies" because they're insincere. While fauxpologies take many forms, two common ones include underdoing or overdoing the expression of remorse. When you underdo remorse, you often give an apology while smuggling in justifications that call into question whether you're genuinely sorry. "I'm a comedian who pushes boundaries," said Shane Gillis in an apology for making racist and homophobic comments. "I'm happy to apologize to anyone who's actually offended by anything I've said. My intention is never to hurt anyone but I am trying to be the best comedian I can and sometimes that requires risks." This statement incorporated elements of an ifpology (by suggesting the offense may not have been real) and of a butpology (by citing good intentions). Yet it also lacked remorse. By twice mentioning his need to push boundaries and take risks as a comedian, Gillis conveyed little, if any, regret. If Gillis genuinely felt the need to make racist and homophobic jokes to be an excellent comedian, we would have preferred a respectful disagreement to an inauthentic apology.

Other fauxpologies blow up the entire apology with another act or comment. In response to allegations he'd sexually harassed four women, celebrity chef Mario Batali published what seemed like the start of a passable apology in his newsletter. "I am so very sorry that I have disappointed my friends, my family, my fans and my team. My behavior was wrong and there are no excuses. I take full responsibility," he wrote. "I will work every day to regain your respect and trust." At the end of the post, however, Batali blew it all up: "P.S. In case you're searching for a holiday-inspired breakfast, these Pizza Dough Cinnamon Rolls are a fan favorite." He added a picture of the rolls and a link to the recipe.

Less intuitively, you can also offer a fauxpology by overdoing the remorse. Diversity consultant Lily Zheng notes that some individuals "go on and on, saying things like: 'I am so sorry. I feel so terrible. . . . What must you think of me?'" As Zheng points out, such melodrama makes matters worse because it pressures the other person to comfort and reassure you. Remember the "ring theory" we discussed in Principle 2 (Build Resilience): comfort in, dump out. One of our students, who is gender nonbinary, gave a stellar presentation for a class assignment about how to create more inclusive learning spaces. They encouraged others not to over-apologize for misgendering trans individuals, noting that after a certain point, the trans person ends up taking care of the apologizer. They advised: "A simple sorry is all you need to say."

Remorse isn't characterized by any particular form of words. What's important is that you mean what you say. We think actor Hank Azaria nailed it when he apologized for voicing the role of Apu in *The Simpsons*. Azaria, who is white, played the South Asian cartoon character for three decades until he stepped down following criticism that the character traded on racial and ethnic stereotypes. Much like the show's creator Matt Groening, Azaria's "first reaction was to bristle" at criticism of Apu. "We make fun of everyone," he said. "Don't tell me how to be funny." But he challenged himself to grow past his own defensiveness. He knew from his recovery from alcoholism that when his feelings were "at their peak," he needed to "shut up," "process those feelings," and "listen and learn." "I read and I talked to people, I talked to a lot of Indian people," Azaria said. "I took seminars. I read." One of his conversations was with an Indian student at his son's school, who hadn't seen *The Simpsons* but knew of Apu because "it's practically a slur at this point." With tears in his eyes, the student begged Azaria to "tell the writers in Hollywood that what they do and what they come up with really matters in people's lives." In a discussion with an Indian American podcaster, Monica Padman, Azaria continued: "I said to him and I'm going to say to you right now: I really do apologize. I know you weren't asking for that, but it's important. I apologize for my part in creating that and participating in that. Part of me feels like I need to go around to every single Indian person in this country and personally apologize."

## Redress (No Talkpologies)

During the racial justice uprisings of 2020, elected officials and corporations in Charlotte, North Carolina, gave thoughtful apologies for the city's role in perpetuating racism and made written commitments to drive policy reform. The mayor stated: "We apologize to the African Americans who came before us and to those living in our city today. Our apology is grounded in the fact that Charlotte is a tale of two cities—we have great prosperity and great poverty." Yet as the *Charlotte Observer* reported six months later, some activists felt little had changed. "It's not enough to say 'I apologize,'" noted Corine Mack, a board member of a local racial justice organization, Restorative Justice CLT. "The way you heal the wrong is to correct the harm that was done."

The final component of an effective apology is redress—taking tangible steps to repair the damage. We call an apology without redress a "talkpology." As author Stephen Covey says, you can't talk your way out of a problem you behaved your way into. Unsurprisingly, research indicates that pairing a statement of apology with redress is more likely to lead to forgiveness than offering a statement alone.

The challenge with redress is that it can require substantial time and energy. Before he came to law school, a student researcher at our center, David Hamburger, ran an apology workshop as part of an employment skills class for people receiving government benefits. He gave students the opportunity to draft their own apologies to people in their life they had hurt, and to read the drafts aloud to the group. One student, Nathan, read a heartfelt apology to the class and concluded with the words "and I'm done." Another student shot back: "You haven't done *shit*." "Talk is cheap," a third student added. "It doesn't matter how eloquent you are if you don't change your behavior."

Hamburger felt these critics were too harsh on Nathan, who may simply have meant he was done reading the apology, not done with the process of repair. But the classroom skirmish led to a productive discussion about redress. Hamburger emphasized to his students that in real life, an apology is usually a dialogue, not a monologue. The apologizer and the recipient collaborate to chart a path forward for the relationship that works for both sides. In later classes, he emphasized that the words of an apology were only one step in a "much longer process." He would frequently write the word "AND" in big letters on the whiteboard and invite participants to brainstorm what actions they could take in addition to saying sorry, such as periodically checking in with the injured party to see how that person felt about the offender's post-apology behavior.

The long-lived obligation created by an apology may make it harder to give. Molly Howes observes that after you offer an apology, you may find yourself asking: "What is enough?" "Shouldn't she be past it by now?" or "Will I ever be out of the doghouse?" But remember that the harm to the other person has often accumulated over a long period. For that reason, redress may take a while too. As Howes counsels, "You may need to build up your resilience for a longer haul than you anticipated."

Again, we draw inspiration from those who get it right. Television host Nick Cannon made amends after he fanned the flames of antisemitism in a conversation with rapper Professor Griff. Cannon had floated conspiracy theories about "illuminati, the Zionists, the Rothschilds," and had claimed that Black people "can't be antisemitic when we are the Semitic people." "That's our birthright," he had noted. "We are the true Hebrews." After the ensuing criticism, Cannon offered his "deepest and most sincere apologies to my Jewish sisters and brothers for the hurtful and divisive words that came out of my mouth." He added: "They reinforced the worst stereotypes of a proud and magnificent people and I feel ashamed of the uninformed and naïve place that these words came from." Noting that he'd received a "minor history lesson" in the days after his comments, he promised to continue learning from rabbis and other Jewish community leaders and institutions.

One such learning experience was a conversation Cannon hosted on his podcast with Rabbi Abraham Cooper. During that conversation, Cannon shared his misgivings about the language of apology: "You can say sorry many times. But if you don't learn, if you're not corrected, and then you move forward, there's no growth, there's no healing. . . . I'd rather sit down with someone of your stature to really correct me." Cannon learned not only from Rabbi Cooper, but from a series of conversations with Jewish advocacy groups and from books on antisemitism. Reflecting on his experience working with Cannon, Rabbi Noam Marans of the American Jewish Committee noted: "In other incidents of celebrities expressing antisemitic comments, we have heard some utter a formulaic text expressing regret and a desire to grow. Cannon did not follow that pattern." He described how Cannon had spent substantial time learning about Jewish people and Judaism and was committed to "undoing the damage he has caused." As Cannon himself put it: "In Hebrew they call it, you know, 'Teshuva,' the process of not only . . . repenting, but through that, if you're ever met with a similar situation that you make a different decision."

TV producer Megan Amram also modeled how to offer redress after writing offensive tweets about Asian Americans, LGBTQ+ people, and people with disabilities. Her apology is a meditation on the power of words and actions. She wrote that an apology "means nothing without action and change behind it," and pledged to use her platform and her job to "foster diverse writers, combat workplace discrimination, educate myself, donate," and vocally support underrepresented groups. After taking a hiatus from social media to reflect and consider "concrete steps I could take," she pledged to use her large platform on social media to "bring awareness and support to those doing all types of amazing work on race, LGBTQ, and disability issues," and to amplify foundations and charities to which she had financially committed. Her subsequent posts have repeatedly highlighted Asian American writers, charities, and industry organizations, spoken out against anti-Asian hate crimes, and encouraged her million-plus followers to support individuals and organizations working on disability and LGBTQ+ rights.

## Applying a Growth Mindset to Apologies

In the TV series *The Unbreakable Kimmy Schmidt*, a white actor plays a Native American character who initially passes as white. The character comes to reclaim her Lakota heritage in ways intended to be tongue-in-cheek, such as howling at the moon when she sees a Native American school mascot. This representation frustrated some Native Americans, who felt the show should have either hired a Native American actor to play the role or rewritten the character to avoid this subplot. Comedian Tina Fey, who cocreated the series, rejected the criticism: "My new goal is not to explain jokes. I feel like we put so much effort into writing and crafting everything, they need to speak for themselves. There's a real culture of demanding apologies, and I'm opting out of that." As fans of Fey, we balked a little to hear her take such a blanket stance against apologies.

A few years later, Fey raised hackles again when she did a sketch on *Saturday Night Live* in the wake of white supremacist rallies in Charlottesville, Virginia. She acknowledged "a lot of us are feeling anxious and we're asking ourselves, 'What can I do? I'm just one person—what can I do?'" She then suggested the right response was to binge-eat a sheet cake, which she capably demonstrated on set. At the time, we chuckled along with the sketch. Yet critics pointed out she was encouraging a passive response to violence against the Black community.

Addressing the controversy in an interview with television host David Letterman, Fey observed: "I felt like a gymnast who did, like, a very solid routine and broke her ankle on the landing. Because it's literally within the last, I think, two or three sentences of the piece that I chunked it." Fey felt that "the implication was that I was telling people to give up and not be active and to not fight—that was not my intention, obviously." She repeated her claim that "I have decided that the culture of apology is not for me." Nevertheless, she said: "What I do is I promise, I swear to God, anyone who has met me, I hear you and I will learn."

In 2020, Fey sparked another race-based controversy, this time involving several episodes of her show *30 Rock* that featured actors in blackface. The episodes came under renewed scrutiny during the resurgence of Black Lives Matter protests that summer. "As we strive to do the work and do better in regards to race in America, we believe that these episodes featuring actors in race-changing makeup are best taken out of circulation," she wrote. "I understand now that 'intent' is not a free pass for white people to use these images. I apologize for pain they have caused. Going forward, no comedy-loving kid needs to stumble on these tropes and be stung by their ugliness. I thank NBCUniversal for honoring this request."

A skeptic could see Fey's path as one of a celebrity harangued into submission. Yet from our perspective, she took a laudable journey. Fey initially sought to "opt out" of a culture of apology. We don't think that's possible. Given that we all make mistakes in conversations about identity, none of us can fairly withdraw from trying to correct those errors. By the sheet cake episode, Fey had moved from a mentality that "the work stands on its own" to a promise to "hear" and "learn." Yet she still fell prey to the common error of excusing herself with intent—"that was not my intention, obviously." In her 2020 comments, she noted that intent wasn't "a free pass" and offered a model apology. She recognized the harm of blackface to comedy-loving kids, took responsibility for causing pain, exhibited remorse, and engaged in redress by using her clout to have the episodes removed.

So now we can admire Fey even more, as she's not only a brilliant comedian, but a person who showed us how to grow.

## Principle 5 **TAKEAWAYS**

- An effective apology contains the "four Rs" of recognition, responsibility, remorse, and redress.

- Recognition means acknowledging the harm. Don't use "ifpologies" such as "I'm sorry if I did anything wrong" or "I'm sorry if you're upset."

- Responsibility means accepting you caused the harm. Don't use "butpologies" such as "I'm sorry, but I was having a miserable day," "I'm sorry, but I didn't mean it," or "I'm sorry, but I'm not a racist."

- Remorse means expressing genuine contrition for causing harm. Don't offer "fauxpologies" by underdoing the remorse with a tepid apology or overdoing the remorse by berating yourself.

- Redress means taking action to correct the harm. Don't offer "talkpologies" by saying sorry without fixing the problem you caused or changing your practices.

# Principle 6:

## Apply the Platinum Rule

During the first summer of the coronavirus pandemic, the Orosa and Chan families were celebrating a birthday at a restaurant in Carmel Valley, California. They sat near a tech CEO, Michael Lofthouse. According to the families, Lofthouse started spewing racist abuse at them, leading Jordan Chan to lift a phone from the table and train its camera on him.

What then unfolded was captured on a video that later went viral. The recording begins with Chan speaking to Lofthouse: "Say that again." Lofthouse doesn't respond. "Oh, now you're shy?" she asks. Lofthouse sticks his middle finger up at her, adding: "That's what I'm saying." He then stands up and says, "You fuckers need to leave! . . . Asian piece of shit." "Oh my God," Chan responds in shock.

At that point, a server at the restaurant—a white woman named Gennica Cochran—intervenes. Planting her body between the families and Lofthouse, she yells: "Right now! Get out of here! Get out!" Lofthouse mutters that he has paid and is about to leave.

"You do not talk to our guests like that! Get out now!" Cochran shouts. As he keeps objecting, Cochran swings her arms like a referee ejecting a player from a game. He finally gathers his belongings and shuffles away. "I did what anybody else should or would do in that situation," Cochran said brightly in a TV interview. "If you see something, do something. Stand up against racism and hatred in any form any time you can."

Cochran's modest claim that "anybody" would have behaved as she did was wishful. A few weeks after the Carmel Valley incident, one of our colleagues, an Asian American woman named Lisa, attended a family gathering with her white husband, Victor, and his extended family. At one point during an otherwise cordial get-together, Victor's cousin Mark started recounting his family's experience during the pandemic and referred to COVID-19 as "the China virus." To ensure no one missed his reference, Mark emphasized: "And yes, I *am* going to call it that." Lisa was the only person of Asian descent at the gathering. She'd witnessed how epithets like "the China virus" and "Kung flu" had stoked anti-Asian hatred during the pandemic. Surely someone—anyone—would challenge Mark's comment? No one did. Surrounded by family, she felt alone. Afterward, Victor asked Lisa if she was angry at Mark. "No," Lisa said. "I'm angry at you for not speaking up. He doesn't know any better. You do."

These scenes show the difference an ally's presence or absence can make. They also involve a more profound sense of allyship than the one we've used until now. As we noted at the outset, allyship takes two forms: "doing no harm" and "doing good." Until now, this book has focused on minimizing harm. We've largely set our sights on improving your behavior in conversations that come to you. Yet allyship can also entail going out into the world to "do good," as Gennica Cochran did. In this more active form of allyship, you leverage your power as an ally to foster a more inclusive culture for the people around you. You're a non-Jewish person who speaks up when you overhear an antisemitic slur hurled at a Jewish person on the bus, a male high-school athlete who intervenes when your teammates make sexist comments about the girls' soccer team, or a socioeconomically privileged student who lobbies your college to admit more students from low-income families.

Some progressives seek to capture this more active sense of allyship with new labels. They reserve the term "ally" for the basic sense of a privileged person of good will, while preferring terms like "upstander," "accomplice," "advocate," or "coconspirator" for the more advanced sense. When Massachusetts senator Elizabeth Warren joined a conversation with Black women activists, she said: "I'm here today as an ally, but can we really just say coconspirator?" The worry that "ally" sounds too passive or superficial has led other progressives to move away from the term altogether. Our own institution, NYU, has replaced its annual "Ally Week" with "Solidarity Week," noting that "solidarity" reflects a stronger commitment to others. Activist Kim Tran has gone so far as to declare "the end of allyship" and the beginning of a "new era of solidarity."

We continue to use "allyship," which is still by far the most common term to describe both the "do no harm" and "do good" forms of support. The word "ally" comes from the Latin "to bind together," which suggests the opposite of disengagement. We acknowledge that allyship can be shallow, performative, or insufficiently attentive to systemic issues. But we believe those are critiques of bad forms of allyship, not of allyship itself.

To be an effective ally in this more demanding sense, you'll need to stack two more principles on top of the ones you've learned so far. The first requires you to think deeply about your relationship to the person you're trying to help, whom we call the "affected person." We address that topic in this chapter. The second principle requires you to consider your relationship to the person who caused the harm, whom we call a "source of non-inclusive behavior." We address that topic in the next and final chapter.

⟡

Our friend Naomi is a white ally who works for a charitable organization. Her white male boss recently decided to establish a committee to address issues of diversity, inclusion, and racial equity. Naomi feared that if the mostly white leaders didn't structure committee meetings carefully, they would exclude the voices of people of color. She read some antiracism resources on how to elicit diverse perspectives and shared some recommendations with her boss. He agreed with her suggestions and urged her to announce her ideas at the next all-company meeting.

After the meeting, a few colleagues approached Naomi to congratulate her on the formation of the committee. She noticed they were all white, and wondered how her non-white colleagues felt. She wasn't left in suspense. Comments poured into her inbox from colleagues of color: "Why did you make that announcement?" "People of color should lead an antiracist initiative, not a white woman." "You could have spoken to us before coming up with this plan." Naomi felt distraught and conflicted. She felt the force of the criticism: "I should have consulted the people I was trying to help." At the same time, she held fast to her initial instinct: "I thought the whole point of allyship was not to burden others with this work."

Naomi encountered the core tension in any ally's relationship to an affected person—the champion/assistant dilemma. In the champion model, the ally's role is to wield their privilege to make the far-reaching change that affected people would struggle to make on their own. Supporters of this model point out that affected people are tired from decades of fighting their own battles and educating people about their identities. Allies can shoulder some of that burden, freeing marginalized people to spend less time advocating for themselves and more time living their lives.

In the assistant model, allies serve as helpers on projects led by others. Proponents of this model point out that affected people know best how to advance their own interests. For that reason, allies need to step back and "pass the mic" to affected people. To the extent allies bring their own ideas and voices to the table, it's in a clearly subordinate role. Writer Caitlin Deen Fair says an ally should be a "backup singer to the movement" they seek to support: "Our only job lies in listening, aiding as requested, and stepping aside when suggested." As our NYU colleague and philosopher Kwame Anthony Appiah observes, this model requires allies to "submit to the direction of the marginalized group, like deferential guests in someone else's home."

While these models are often in tension, they're not inherently contradictory. Some situations call for allies to step up while others call for them to step back. At a campus forum we hosted on the #MeToo movement, a woman in the audience gestured at the room filled almost exclusively with women and asked, "Where are the men?" Yet the same woman would have been rightly annoyed if men had surged into the room and commandeered the forum.

The choice whether to be a "champion" or an "assistant" can be thorny, and we sometimes struggle to manage that dilemma in our own lives. We can't offer hard-and-fast rules. What we can offer is a tool to grapple with the question, sometimes called the Platinum Rule. You're probably familiar with the Golden Rule: treat others as you would wish to be treated. When applying that idea to allyship, it's critical to remember the other person is *not* like you along potentially important dimensions. So the Platinum Rule enhances the Golden Rule by urging you to help others as *they* would wish to be helped. It reminds you to take the other person's preference seriously, whether by asking directly or by carefully reflecting on their needs. If you heed it, the rule will give you more confidence in your choice to be a champion, an assistant, or something in between.

## Mind Your Motives

It's the scene in *To Kill a Mockingbird* beloved by many. The lawyer Atticus Finch has just watched an all-white jury wrongly convict his Black client Tom Robinson of raping a white woman. Atticus packs his papers into his briefcase and leaves the courtroom— defeated but unbowed. Atticus's young daughter, Scout, watches the trial from the balcony, which is also the "colored" section of the courtroom. She's mesmerized by her father's "lonely walk down the aisle" until she gets a punch on the arm from the town's reverend. She looks up to see all the Black people in the balcony standing in a silent ovation for her father. The reverend tells her to rise too: "Your father's passing."

This scene represents a classic vision of allyship. Though we grew up in different generations and countries, we both remember being riveted by this moment when we first read Harper Lee's novel as high-school students. We were young enough that it shaped our consciousness of social justice. We were also young enough that we never questioned the troubling aspects of the scene.

Sociologist Matthew Hughey explores those undertones in describing the 1962 film adaptation of *To Kill a Mockingbird* as "one of the first white savior films." As Hughey explains, a white savior film is a movie in which a white individual rescues a non-white individual or group from a bleak fate. The genre is robust—Hughey canvasses fifty such films over a quarter century, including *Glory, Dances with Wolves, Dangerous Minds, Amistad, Finding Forrester, The Last Samurai, Gran Torino, Avatar, The Blind Side,* and *The Help.* These films position the white savior next to two sets of stock characters. On one side are the "bad whites," who are bigoted and violent. On the other side are the "natives," who are "too desolate or captive to their own circumstances to help themselves." The white savior liberates the natives from the bad whites, armed with exactly the right morals and "redemptive je ne sais quoi."

In a rollicking parody of this genre, the TV show *Late Night with Seth Meyers* released a trailer for a fake movie titled *White Savior.* Set in the Jim Crow era, the film portrays a Black woman, Loretta Washington, who became "a world-renowned scientist, an accomplished cellist, and activist." The main character, however, is Seth Meyers's Jack—"a man who was white while she did it." Throughout the trailer, Jack tries to serve as Loretta's ally, sowing catastrophe at every turn. As Loretta is about to make a speech, Jack adjusts her microphone and says: "Her mic was too high but I fixed it. It's fixed because of me." He never consults Loretta before swashbuckling in to help her. When racists harass her in a bar, Jack interrupts her deft response with his own ham-fisted one. When Loretta defiantly enters a whites-only restroom, he launches into a diatribe against the scandalized white women assembled outside in pastel suits and elbow gloves. Embarrassed, Loretta yells: "I can't go with you standing out there!" Later in the trailer, a white woman tries to adopt Loretta, saying Loretta "will no longer want for anything in this world." "Adopt me?" Loretta asks quizzically. "I'm older than you!" The clip is a master class on how allies can fail the people they seek to help.

Saviorism is a common impulse. A disability advocate identifies "approaching disabled people like a missionary" as a top allyship mistake. Experts on male allyship in the workplace warn of the "fake male feminist" who "slings on feminism like a superhero cape when his boss is watching."

People from nondominant groups widely deride the savior mentality. Among other critiques, they call it out as "virtue signaling" (needing others to see how good you are) or "cookie seeking" (needing others to praise or affirm you). As racial justice advocate Nova Reid notes, this motivation "serves primarily to satisfy ego," putting the would-be ally's "actions and intentions over and above the cause." A healthier motivation for allyship is an intrinsic one—you believe it's the right thing to do. A test of whether you have proper motivations is simply to ask: *Am I making this more about myself than about the people I'm trying to help?*

You might wonder why an ally's motive matters. A nonprofit organization usually doesn't care if people donate out of pure altruism or because they want to feel a warm inner glow. But unlike a charitable donation, which is interchangeable with any comparable donation, conversations are intensely personal. In one study, researcher Charles Chu asked Black participants to react to a scenario in which a white ally confronted the source of a racist comment. Participants who thought the ally confronted the bias for extrinsic reasons (such as to "impress" them) were more likely to feel disempowered by the intervention. And just as affected people distrust allies with extrinsic motivations, they trust allies with intrinsic ones. A separate study looked at white people nominated as allies by people of color and found them high in intrinsic motivation.

Motives also matter because extrinsic motivation can lead to what's sometimes called "allyship fatigue." Allyship is frequently challenging. You're bucking the status quo and putting yourself in uncomfortable situations. You're also opening yourself to criticism that you've intervened unhelpfully, as Naomi found. If you're serving as an ally only to look good, you'll be tempted to quit when the trophies stop arriving.

More than half a century after the release of the film, playwright Aaron Sorkin adapted *To Kill a Mockingbird* for Broadway. He too loved the scene where the Black observers stand reverently as Atticus leaves the courtroom. But he distrusted his own instinct: "That really is a white savior moment. And it's a liberal fantasy that marginalized people will recognize me. That I'm one of the good ones. Not only isn't it a moment I wanted to have in the play but I turned it upside down." In Sorkin's play, Atticus is bewildered by his Black housekeeper Calpurnia's "passive aggressive" behavior toward him. He pesters her about what's bothering her, to no avail. At the end of the play, Calpurnia finally reveals she disliked how Atticus sought credit from her after he agreed to represent Tom Robinson: "You told me and I guess I didn't react with sufficient gratitude and as I walked away, you said, under your breath, 'You're welcome.' And I never thought . . . this house would be a place I'd have to remember to be grateful." This seemingly small change vastly complicates and enriches Atticus as a character. He shifts from being a paragon to being someone who struggles like the rest of us to mind his motives.

## Consider Whether the Affected Person Wants Help

Allies frequently hold back because they worry it's not their place to meddle in another person's business. Particularly when feeling discomfort, they return to their factory settings of passivity and avoidance. If that sounds like you, we want to set your default in the other direction. You've already absorbed the foundational principles that will make you a more adept ally than most. First, you learned to beware the four conversational traps of avoid, deflect, deny, and attack. Then you got into the right emotional and intellectual state for these dialogues by building resilience and cultivating curiosity. Finally, you learned how to disagree respectfully and apologize authentically. Armed with these skills, you can proceed with confidence in most situations, as Gennica Cochran did at her restaurant.

This advice comes with an important caveat. Before helping, pause to consider whether the person wants help at all. Social scientists have found that affected people can feel downcast when they receive unsolicited help without any evidence of need. One foundational study found that Black students who received unsolicited help from white peers on a word puzzle reported lower self-esteem about their own competence than Black students who didn't receive such help or white students who did. Another study in Israel found that Arab students felt worse about themselves when Jewish research assistants provided unsolicited help on a test. As these studies suggest, when you help someone across a power dynamic, you risk unintentionally implying they can't hack it on their own.

In most allyship situations, you can consider whether the affected person will welcome your help without posing the question directly. You'll often find it awkward, embarrassing, or downright impossible to ask them. We think of a male board chair who was running a university meeting. One of the senior faculty members boasted that the research assistants in his department were "the most beautiful women at the university." While the comment warranted a response, it would have been ridiculous for the chair to poll the women in the room to check if they wanted his help. The

Platinum Rule enabled him to go it alone, as he could infer that many women would want him to intervene. He adroitly spoke up on his own behalf rather than attempting to speak on theirs: "I'm concerned that in this day and age such comments about women are still being made." The faculty member turned pale and apologized.

Sometimes, however, you won't be sure whether your help is welcome, and nothing will prevent you from asking. In such cases, go ahead and ask. Naomi didn't know whether the people of color at her organization wanted her assistance in establishing an anti-racism committee. Unlike the chair of the university board meeting, she could have sought guidance, such as by approaching some colleagues of color privately to let them know she was thinking of setting up the antiracism initiative. She could even have made her own dilemma explicit: "I don't think the responsibility of addressing racial inequity in a majority-white organization should be yours to carry. But if you're willing, I'd like to get your input now in case you'd prefer to take the lead or structure the initiative differently from what I had in mind." Had she taken this approach, the affected people might have turned down her help, or given her useful feedback.

Another important reason for asking whether your help is welcome comes from the opposite direction. Sometimes the problem is not that you're barreling in to provide unsolicited help, but that you're not providing help at all. Affected people might want your help but feel too embarrassed to request it because they don't want to be a burden. Shaniqua, a low-income student at an elite college, observed that growing up homeless had taught her to be grateful for whatever she received: "Someone gives you a shirt, even if it's ugly, you wear it." That mentality, she said, had made it "hard . . . to advocate for" herself in college: "Part of me is like,

'I've been given enough.'" Another low-income student, Rosalind, felt the same way. Despite experiencing a concussion that caused serious problems with double vision, memory, concentration, and sleep, she coped on her own for over a month until she finally went to her residential advisor and broke down in tears. "I thought I could do it on my own," she said. "I don't like asking for help."

It's not just socioeconomic disadvantage that causes people to shy away from requesting help. United States Supreme Court justice Sonia Sotomayor was "embarrassed" about her diabetes when diagnosed as a child: "I thought it showed weakness. I thought my friends would make fun of it. And so I hid it." While hosting a party in her thirties, she collapsed on her bed from dangerously low blood sugar levels. "My friends didn't know what was happening, 'cause I had never told them. And so I almost died in a room full of people who love me." That experience prompted her to be more open about her diabetes. It also inspired her to write a children's book decades later titled *Just Ask!*. The book, she says, encourages readers to look at the people in their lives who have disabilities or "do things differently" and ask them when they need help: "Find out how it affects them and how you can help and when. 'Cause I don't need help all the time, but I do sometimes, and people should know that. And you should know that about the people you love and care about."

When you ask affected people whether they want support, they'll sometimes say no. Although rejection can sting, keep in mind it's still a victory for allyship. Allies are often invisible to the people they seek to help. To overcome that invisibility in the LGBTQ+ context, many workplaces give out rainbow pins, flags, and stickers so supporters of the community can "come out" as allies. An offer of help can perform the same function. By asking if you can be an ally, you show you notice and care. The affected people who decline your support today have banked you for the future. A week, a month, or a year from now, they can return to you for help.

## Consider Whether the Affected Person Wants *This Kind* of Help

Mary is a blind woman who uses a white cane to navigate her commute to work. One day, she finds a construction project obstructing her usual path to the bus stop. Stopping at a street corner, Mary asks passersby to confirm that the bus stop is one block away. One pedestrian tells her it's too dangerous for her to be walking on her own, takes her by the arm, and insists on accompanying her to her destination. Another pedestrian says it's too dangerous for her to be walking on her own and tells her to go home. Which pedestrian was more helpful?

As psychologist Katie Wang and her colleagues discovered in a study based on this hypothetical situation, the answer you give may depend on whether you're sighted. In Wang's study, the sighted participants thought the zealous response (taking Mary to her destination) was significantly better than the hostile one (telling Mary to go home). In contrast, the blind participants rated the zealous and hostile reactions to be almost equally inappropriate. The zealous help, like the hostile refusal, still didn't give Mary the help she requested—directions to the bus stop. It also suggested Mary was incompetent at navigating her environment.

Unhelpful help abounds in other contexts as well. Younger people can use "elderspeak"—the patronizing mode of address that treats older people as childlike. In a study of elderspeak in dementia-care settings, researchers found that when nurses used terms like "honey" or "good girl" to refer to their patients or made statements like "Are we ready for our bath?" the patients were more likely to reject the help by saying no, turning away, or kicking. Like Mary, the patients needed the help, but the form of help was demeaning.

Such mistakes can pile up on a grand scale when allies join social justice movements. In the case of Black Lives Matter, it was clear the Black community needed allies to stand in solidarity with them. In responding to that call, some allies acted with empathy, wisdom, and grace. Others . . . not so much.

Perhaps most infamously, Pepsi made a television commercial showing protestors facing off against the police. The spot opens with a group of marchers holding signs that read "Peace" and "Join the Conversation." Despite the generic slogans, the setup unmistakably refers to the racial protests of the time. At the climactic moment, reality television star Kendall Jenner, who is white, walks up to one of the police officers and hands him a can of Pepsi. He accepts it with a smile and drinks it, leading to rejoicing and reconciliation.

Rarely has an ad been panned more swiftly and deservedly. Critics felt Pepsi trivialized the real danger protestors experienced at the hands of police. Some contrasted the image of Jenner cozying up to the cops with the real-life image of Ieshia Evans, a Black woman who stood serenely and fearlessly while being charged by police in riot gear. Bernice King, the daughter of Martin Luther King Jr., posted a photograph of her father in a confrontation with the police accompanied by the caption: "If only Daddy would have known about the power of #Pepsi." Pepsi pulled the ad and issued an apology. Jenner also apologized.

Jenner was not the only aspiring ally to draw ire for her unwelcome assistance to the movement. *Riverdale* actor Lili Reinhart posted a topless photograph of herself on Instagram with the caption: "Now that my sideboob has gotten your attention, Breonna Taylor's murderers have not been arrested. Demand justice." Taylor was a Black woman who had been fatally shot by police officers in her own home. The backlash to Reinhart's post was also scathing. One world-weary observer of the zeitgeist wrote: "We have entered a thrilling transitional phase in which the celebs have resumed thirst posting but have not yet stopped social justice posting, resulting in wondrous juxtapositions like this one." Such misjudgment, of course, knows no gender. Social media influencer Benno Peters posted a photo on Instagram showcasing his washboard abs with the caption "Rest in Peace George Floyd!" As one commenter noted: "Fair message, but the picture is cringe." The allyship photo shoot grew into such a genre that *Glamour* magazine published an article with the tag: "Historic antiracist uprisings are not your opportunity to look cute on the feed."

Alongside celebrities and soda companies, ordinary individuals also missed the mark. In the wake of George Floyd's murder, millions posted plain black squares on their social media pages with the tag #BlackLivesMatter as part of a "blackout" to express solidarity with protestors. Yet such allyship made it harder for activists to use the hashtag to amplify messages, boost organizations accepting donations, or share resources for those in need without drowning in a sea of black squares. "Posting a black square" quickly became a meme for "performative" or "optical" allyship. As Ben Platt's character on the television series *The Premise* says: "I've really done everything I can think of to do, OK? I posted that black square, I deleted that black square, I reposted the black square, and then I redeleted the black square. And literally nothing is ever enough!"

Even the Spanish postal service caused an allyship kerfuffle when it issued "equality stamps" in a spectrum of skin tones on the one-year anniversary of Floyd's murder. To "send a message against racial inequality," stamps with darker shades had lower values. While acknowledging the postal service's good intentions, a Spanish expert on race pronounced the campaign "an absolute disaster." He pointed out the contradiction of issuing "stamps with a different value depending on the color in order to show the equal value of our lives." The service yanked the stamps soon after.

To be fair, allyship errors often stem from an admirable impulse toward action. Responding to critics of his torso pic, Peters quoted Martin Luther King Jr.: "In the end, we will remember not the words of our enemies, but the silence of our friends." Yes, the greater threat in allyship situations is hapless passivity, not thoughtless activity. But also, it's wrong to think any help is better than no help.

All these would-be allies to the Black Lives Matter movement didn't fully consider whether the affected people wanted the specific form of help they extended. Had they applied the Platinum Rule, they might have asked whether the form of help they chose could make light of the issues (by suggesting racialized police violence could be solved with a can of soda), focus undue attention on themselves (by revealing sexualized bits of their anatomy), impede more meaningful forms of allyship (by swamping communication channels with black squares), or send the wrong message (by suggesting darker skin tones have lower value).

You already have the tools to avoid giving people the wrong form of help. You could follow the "ring theory" we discussed in Principle 2 (Build Resilience) by enlisting other allies in your community to provide input and support. You could also follow our advice from Principle 3 (Cultivate Curiosity) to study the relevant issues. Merely reading online resources on "how to support the Black Lives Matter movement" would have steered allies away from many of the more cringeworthy interventions. Finally, when you're trying to help a specific affected person such as Mary at the bus stop, you could simply ask them what help they want, as we've recommended in this chapter.

Even when you've applied all these tools, you may encounter a wrinkle—you disagree with the approach the affected person asks you to take. Suppose they want you to condemn a perpetrator of bias in a public forum, but you think a private conversation would be more productive. In such situations, we encourage you to share your perspective with the affected person using the rules of disagreement we outlined in Principle 4 (Disagree Respectfully). You might persuade the other person your approach would be better, or they may persuade you. If you remain convinced of your position but the affected person won't budge, don't steamroll over them. Remember that the ultimate goal is to help people as they wish to be helped. Right or wrong, the affected person has an interest in making their own choices. At an impasse, the appropriate response is to opt out: "I'm sorry, I don't think I'm your best ally in this situation." You can always work together in the future when you're better aligned.

## Consider Systemic Solutions

Knowing that professors tend to call on men more than on women in class, Kenji had for many years tried to be careful about gender dynamics in his teaching. Yet when he conducted an audit of his own classroom practices, he realized he was still disproportionately calling on men. Filled with chagrin, he resolved to do better as an ally to the women in his courses. For a few lectures, he did. But as the semester wore on, he noticed that when he got tired or stressed or particularly excited about the material he was teaching, he'd relapse into his bad habits.

We know from research that bias is sticky. When you're laser-focused on it, you can counteract it. But once your attention wanders, the bias reasserts itself. Social psychologists Mahzarin Banaji and Anthony Greenwald compare fighting implicit bias (popularly referred to as "unconscious bias") to pulling on a rubber band. You can stretch your mind to think less stereotypically if you exercise special care. When you relax, though, your biases snap back into place.

All is not lost. Behavioral economist Iris Bohnet offers a solution: focus more on changing systems than on changing minds. Bohnet uses orchestra screens as a key example. In 1970, women composed only 5 percent of musicians in the top five orchestras in the United States. Now they're more than 35 percent. Researchers attribute this dramatic increase in part to a simple design fix: the orchestras changed their audition process so that musicians performed behind a screen. The gender of the performer became invisible to the orchestra director. Instead of trying to change biased minds, leaders changed the environment in which those minds made decisions. Bohnet explains that similar design solutions are available when interviewing candidates for employment, fostering inclusive teams, or developing government policy.

In fact, Bohnet's book gave Kenji the solution to his problem of calling on men more than on women. He asked his assistant to create a randomized call list for each class. No matter how tired, stressed, or excited he became, he could always read names off a list. This systemic fix proved more effective than any effort he'd made on his own. When he did another audit, he passed easily.

David came to a similar disheartening realization about his own implicit bias while interviewing candidates for student research positions. When our center launched, we had no formal recruitment system in place, so David defaulted to having an open-ended chat with the applicants about their goals, skills, interests, and backgrounds. After conducting a few of these conversations, however, he realized he was drawn to students similar to himself—a common form of implicit bias sometimes known as affinity or "like likes like" bias. One student had spent a year living in David's hometown of Melbourne, which led to a lively conversation about their favorite neighborhoods and restaurants. Thankfully, David realized that "spending time in Melbourne" wasn't a relevant qualification for the role of student researcher. He decided to follow Bohnet's recommendation to conduct "structured" interviews by asking each candidate the same questions in the same order. While it required more planning, this technique reduced the bias that crept into David's open-ended interviews and allowed him to compare candidates to each other against merit-based benchmarks.

Working off call lists or conducting structured interviews may seem limited to narrow situations like teaching or recruiting. But many other systemic solutions are available to use in a wider range of ordinary conversations. When you're leading a group discussion—say, at a parent-teacher association meeting or a team huddle at work—you've got options. You could adopt the "two-two rule" we learned from the organization Black Theatre United, which asks participants to limit their comments to two minutes and then to wait for two other colleagues to speak before jumping in again. You could employ the "check-mark rule" used by some leaders at Google, where you write everyone's name down on a sheet and add a tick next to each person who speaks, enabling you to ensure no one is dominating the conversation and that everyone has an opportunity to contribute. If you're a facilitator inviting contributions from an audience, you could follow Iris Bohnet's "wait-five-seconds rule" after you pose a question so you have a wider pool of volunteers from which to choose, rather than relying on those who are quickest to raise their hand. We've also learned from our student Wenny Shen about conferences adopting the "third-man rule," which asks men to hold their question if they would be the third man in a row to ask one. All these rules take what would otherwise be a free-for-all and add some structure to make the conversation more inclusive.

Don't let us scare you off—in allyship, a one-off fix will often be enough. But if you're dealing with the same inclusion issue over and over again, it's worth considering a systemic solution. Again, the Platinum Rule guides you in this direction: affected people typically prefer systemic fixes over short-lived relief.

If you do embrace a systemic solution, bear in mind that systems amplify both good and bad outcomes. If designed well, they help people at scale. If designed poorly, they spread harm more widely than any individual misstep. You'll need to be extra careful to make sure your systemic solution is working as intended in any given context. Sociologist Anthony Abraham Jack conducted research at an elite university that closed all of its on-campus eateries during spring break. Rich students spent the time backpacking in Europe or skiing in Colorado, while poor students stayed on campus and struggled to find food. The university's Office of Financial Aid adopted a systemic solution, issuing a "guide to budget restaurants." Yet Jack learned of a kink in the system. Students pointed out that the office knew exactly how constrained their finances were, meaning that it should have known that even the "budget" restaurants lay outside their means. Jack offered an alternative solution for the university to consider: keep at least one cafeteria open during spring break.

We had our own recent experience of struggling to devise a systemic solution. Our center hosts an annual speaker series. During the Q&A portion of our first few events, we opened the floor, waited for hands to go up, then passed a roving microphone around the room. Yet we quickly encountered an inclusion issue that anyone who has attended a public event knows well. Time and again, a small number of audience members, most of whom were men, would dominate the discussion. Holding forth for several minutes, they would regale attendees with "more of a comment than a question," leaving little time for the speaker to respond.

This recurring problem called for a systemic fix. So we scrapped the microphones and required audience members to write down questions using index cards and pencils. We then selected the best ones to read out on stage.

Initially, this solution was a triumph—the questions were smarter and shorter. Yet the system soon generated a glitch. At an event we cohosted with the law school's disability student group, students pointed out that attendees with motor impairments might not be able to handwrite questions. They asked if we could revert to the microphone method, and we of course said yes.

You can guess what happened next. As the event opened for Q&A, an attendee seized the microphone and delivered a lecture while other audience members sighed and looked around the room in boredom. The monologue concluded with the line "I don't have a question."

Such difficulties may lead you to feel hopeless—that you "can't win" no matter what you try. We strongly believe, however, that if you apply resilience, you can usually muddle through to a system that works. In our case, we decided that asking for written questions was the most inclusive process overall, so long as we continued to make individual accommodations for people who needed them.

❦

When we give presentations on the topic of allyship, we sometimes poll audiences on their experiences being allies to others and receiving allyship themselves. We start by asking people to reflect on the last time they were an ally and to rate their own effectiveness. They usually think they did a decent job. Then we ask them to reflect on the last time they were an affected person and rate the skill of the allies who supported them. Here the rating tends to go down, which suggests many allies are struggling to implement the Platinum Rule. The lowest results occur when we ask one final question: "Think of the last time you were a source of non-inclusive behavior. Did you have an ally who helped you grow past your mistake?" Here the numbers plummet. Even those who have allies as affected people report lacking allies when they're the source. When they make a mistake, they're left to recover from the error on their own—either because others don't want to help them or don't know how.

We want to close that gap. You've already extended empathy to the affected person by applying the Platinum Rule. To round out your allyship journey, we encourage you to stretch your empathy in one final surprising direction. We invite you to offer help not just to the person harmed by bias, but also to the person who caused the harm.

## Principle 6 **TAKEAWAYS**

- When engaged in more active forms of allyship—seeking to help people affected by bias—apply the Platinum Rule by helping people as they wish to be helped, rather than as you wish to help them.

- Mind your motives. Allyship can involve a "savior" impulse. Try to cultivate an intrinsic motivation—be an ally because it's the right thing to do, not because you expect to receive praise.

- Consider whether the affected person wants help by reflecting on their needs or by asking. Respect their wishes if they say no. Even a refusal of help is a win, because it reveals you as an ally.

- Consider whether the affected person wants your proposed form of help. Some help can be patronizing, trivializing, empty, or counterproductive. If you're unsure, turn to other allies in your community for input, conduct research, or check with the affected person.

- Consider systemic solutions. Be careful: If designed well, systems help people at scale. If designed poorly, they spread harm more widely than individual missteps.

# Principle 7:

## Be Generous to the Source

Our student Melissa and her partner Paul initially struggled with how to respond when Paul was misgendered. People regularly referred to Paul—a trans man—as "ma'am," "she," or "her." After these individuals realized their mistake, they would usually backtrack or apologize clumsily, causing Paul embarrassment.

Together, Melissa and Paul developed a simple system. If a random stranger misgendered Paul, they'd let it go. They didn't see any benefit in correcting someone they'd probably never see again. Friends and family members were another story. When the misgendering seemed like a slip of the tongue, Melissa would casually refer to Paul as "he" and hope the other person would take the hint. When it seemed like the person didn't understand what it meant to be trans, Melissa would wait until Paul had walked away, then have a polite conversation to explain his pronouns. The protocol kept everyone happy—both Paul and the person who misgendered him would avoid the awkwardness of a public confrontation. Of course, it meant more work for Melissa. But as Paul's partner and ally, she was more than willing to play this role.

All their planning was blown to pieces when Melissa brought Paul home for Thanksgiving—the first time she'd introduced him to her extended family. They sat near Melissa's grandfather Harold and her outspoken liberal brother, Ben. Then it happened: Harold used the wrong pronouns to refer to Paul. Melissa had geared up to intervene, when Ben launched into a rant: "That is so transphobic, Grandpa! Melissa used Paul's pronouns earlier when she introduced him to you. You have no excuse! This is how you *always* are. You're *never* supportive!" Paul let out an uncomfortable laugh, but otherwise sat in stunned silence. Melissa was mortified. As Ben continued to bluster, Harold left the room in a huff. In the years since, Melissa and Paul have never been seated next to Harold at a family gathering. Harold now seems to steer well clear of them.

🕊

When you witness non-inclusive behavior, your first instinct may be like Ben's—to condemn the perpetrator for harming a vulnerable person. Reflexive condemnation is enticing because you can confront bad behavior without having to regulate your emotions or choose your words carefully.

Yet Ben's approach was ineffective. At this point, we hope it's clear his intervention failed Paul, as it violated the Platinum Rule. What may be less intuitive is that Ben's actions also failed his grandfather Harold.

The idea that allyship entails obligations to the perpetrator of bias may sound shocking. Most people think of allyship as a two-way relationship between the ally (Ben) and the affected person (Paul). But there's a third party involved in most allyship situations—the source of non-inclusive behavior, or "source" for short (Harold). Putting it all together, there's the ally ("I saw it"), the affected person ("It happened to me"), and the source ("I did it"):

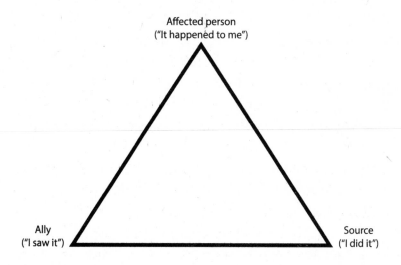

When we showed this triangle to a room full of engineers, a woman stood up and said indignantly: "Why are we wasting our energy worrying about the source of non-inclusive behavior?! That person is the bad actor in the situation. The source *should* be punished or ostracized!" She got a smattering of applause from others in the room. We'd been working with the woman's employer, a large tech company, to develop allyship training. As we started to roll out the concepts, we kept hearing this criticism. Everyone understood the premise of being allies to people affected by bias. But being an ally to the source? That crossed a line.

We knew we had to hone a crisp response to this objection. We huddled for a few weeks and came up with this one: "You should be an ally to the source of non-inclusive behavior because someday the source will be you." The objections dissolved. The ethos of being an ally to the source, not just the affected person, became a distinguishing feature of how this organization approached allyship.

This experience made us realize that when people think about allyship, they usually see themselves sitting permanently in the ally position. But allyship is more like a game of musical chairs. Some days you're the ally, some days you're the affected person, and some days you're the source. In fact, you can cycle through all three positions in a single day.

To internalize this crucial point, please take a moment to move through the triangle. Think of a time when you were an ally. Think of a time when you were the affected person. And finally, think of a time when you were the source. We have yet to meet anyone who can't come up with instances when they occupied each of these roles.

If you look at the world assuming you'll never be the source of non-inclusive behavior, it's much easier to cancel people. If you look at the world assuming you'll sometimes be the source, you'll have a fundamentally different take on how sources should be treated. One leader, Michele, told us she was outraged during the #MeToo movement when men in her workplace reduced contact with women out of fear of saying the wrong thing. She found herself thinking: "You're copping out. Why don't you just try not being offensive, you jerks?!" At a later point, she misgendered a colleague's nonbinary child, and confessed her error to her teenage daughter. Her daughter scoffed that "old people" were essentially the only ones who couldn't "wrap their heads around" pronouns. Michele said this experience prompted a conversation with her daughter about the "importance of keeping up" but also "the importance of understanding and educating, rather than shaming." And critically, Michele connected the dots between her two experiences. This round of musical chairs gave her "a little sympathy" for the men who were scared to engage, even as Michele noted she'd continue to challenge them to do better.

The enlightened self-interest argument—that you will be the source someday—seemed like our best play to persuade the skeptics at the tech company. But more altruistic reasons should also lead you to be an ally to the source. For one, when you're an ally, you're by definition not directly targeted by the source's behavior. As such, you have enough distance from the incident to display greater generosity. If you refuse to educate and rehabilitate the source, you're either placing that burden on affected people or leaving the source to stew alone without the assistance they may need to grow.

Another reason to be generous is that sources are often ignorant rather than malicious. We think here of an older straight white male colleague who regularly used the term "sexual preference" rather than "sexual orientation" in conversations with us. He's adamantly pro-gay, but didn't realize "sexual preference" was an outdated term because it suggests a person's sexuality is a choice. Even full-time diversity and inclusion professionals make these mistakes. In a recent conversation, a professional in our field started to say "disabled" but then corrected herself to say "differently abled," apparently not realizing that "differently abled" was widely considered patronizing within the disability community. We ourselves continued to use the defunct term "preferred pronouns" until someone told us the trans community mostly favored "pronouns," again because gender pronouns are not a matter of personal preference. In instances like these, a rush to judgment can turn a teachable moment into one where the source feels unfairly attacked and starts to ignore feedback. As we've learned from grim experience, individuals otherwise sympathetic to the project of inclusion can be driven by heavy-handed confrontations to become adamantly opposed to it. Scenes like the Thanksgiving tableau with Ben and Harold can turn into villain origin stories.

Finally, you should consider being an ally to the source to acknowledge that people enter these dialogues at different starting points. News anchor Chris Hayes observes: "If you watch a farce, and it's the person at the dinner party who doesn't know which fork to use, that's the person you root for." Unfortunately, as Hayes points out, a significant slice of the population has come to view "genuine struggles for social justice and equality" as "elite manners." Part of that perception comes from judgmental allies who disparage anybody who picks up the wrong conversational fork. Like any habits, the customs of identity conversations are easier to acquire if you had them drilled into you from a young age. It would undermine inclusion to treat someone as a bigot for lacking the background to get the words right in every situation.

Ultimately, we agree with feminist scholar bell hooks, who suggests it's possible to "hold people accountable for wrongdoing" while remaining "in touch with their humanity enough to believe in their capacity to be transformed." Of course, we don't expect you to display endless, unconditional generosity to anyone who behaves inappropriately. As we'll describe later, we think you can opt out of being an ally to the source in a number of situations. But assuming you've decided to be generous in a particular case, we have some ideas on how to go about it.

## Separate the Behavior from the Person

Emory law professor Sasha Volokh was teaching the landmark United States Supreme Court decision of *Snyder v. Phelps*. The case involved the Westboro Baptist Church, a fervently antigay church infamous for its inflammatory placards, such as those reading

"America Is Doomed," "You're Going to Hell," and "God Hates Fags." Church members brandished these signs while protesting a funeral, and the deceased's family sued for "intentional infliction of emotional distress." The Supreme Court rejected the claim, finding that the church had engaged in constitutionally protected free speech.

Volokh introduced the case to his class of first-year law students and noted it concerned "the Westboro Baptist Church— they're the 'God Hates Fags' church." He continued the class with no sense anything was amiss. The next day, however, a student alerted him that other students were planning to complain about his use of the word "fags."

The incident caught fire. Some students condemned Volokh's comment and organized a campus-wide protest. They tied it to two prior incidents at Volokh's law school involving other professors who had used the n-word in class. Others staunchly defended Volokh's behavior as reasonable. Still others criticized the comment but defended his right to make it on free speech grounds.

Taken alone, we think Volokh's behavior was defensible, even if we wouldn't have used the term in teaching the case ourselves. But our interest here isn't in the substance of Volokh's comment, but in how some of his critics challenged him. According to an Emory law student, one professor said to his own class that he was "one-hundred percent sure" Volokh's comment was "a free-speech stunt" where he was "trying to see how much he could get away with." When we spoke with Volokh, he told us a colleague said, "I think you should leave this law school, because you don't care about our community." These comments ascribed negative intent to Volokh, suggesting he was deliberately provocative or callous.

We disagree with this approach. Even when someone's behavior is unequivocally wrong, it's critical to maintain the distinction between what someone does and who someone is. Saying that someone intended to do a bad act or that they don't care about others blurs that distinction. After all, what kind of person deliberately sets out to harm other people?

Our colleague Bryan Stevenson, a prominent legal scholar and activist who defends people imprisoned on death row, regularly says, "I believe that each person is more than the worst thing they've ever done." As he explains: "I think if someone tells a lie, they're not just a liar. If someone takes something, they're not just a thief. I think even if you kill someone, you're not just a killer." Many progressives rightly apply this principle to people who commit crimes, yet forget it in identity conversations.

We believe that's a missed opportunity. Professor of social work Brené Brown distinguishes between guilt and shame, noting that guilt is when someone says "I did something bad," while shame is when someone says "I am bad." Brown argues that guilt is uncomfortable but constructive—it lets you see when your behavior doesn't match who you are. Shame, however, is destructive. It "corrodes the very part of us that believes we can change and do better." We see a deep connection between this analysis and Carol Dweck's work on fixed and growth mindsets. "I am bad" suggests your abilities are fixed. "I did something bad" suggests you remain capable of growth.

The first technique for separating the behavior from the person is to separate intent from impact. We emphasized in Principle 1 (Beware the Four Conversational Traps) and Principle 5 (Apologize Authentically) that when you make a mistake on an identity issue, you shouldn't deflect to your good intentions—your actions can be harmful even if you didn't mean them to be. In a similar vein, we believe you shouldn't infer ill intent from a negative impact. It would be like assuming that anytime someone steps on another person's foot, they did it on purpose. It would also be unfair to accuse sources of bad intentions while not allowing them to cite their good intentions in response.

Separating the source's intent from the impact of their actions is both principled and strategic. It's principled because you rarely know what another person intended. It's also strategic, because it's easy for the source to rebut anything you say about their intent. In contrast, it's hard for them to rebut anything you say about the impact of their actions. If you say to the source, "You made that comment maliciously," you're inviting them to say, "No I didn't." What could you possibly say in response—"I know your intentions better than you do"? Yet if you say, "I was offended by your comment," you're on surer ground. They can't reasonably reply, "That wasn't the impact I had on you." Just as they're the expert on the intent behind their words, you're the expert on how those words landed on you.

Importantly, we don't think you need to swing to the opposite extreme and assume their intentions were good, unless you know the person well enough to be confident in that assessment. You're not required to give everyone the benefit of the doubt. Separating intent from impact makes no assumptions either way.

A related strategy for separating the behavior from the person is to affirm the source as a person while you give feedback on their actions. G. T. Bynum, the white mayor of Tulsa, Oklahoma, got himself into political trouble after police officers fatally shot an unarmed Black man, Terence Crutcher. Crutcher had been on hallucinogenic drugs at the time of the incident. A reporter asked Bynum: "A lot of people saw what happened to Terence Crutcher and they said, 'This wouldn't have happened if he was white.' Do you think that's true?" "No, I don't," the mayor responded. "It is more about the really insidious nature of drug utilization than it is about race, in my opinion." These comments angered many residents of Tulsa, including the Crutcher family. A few days later,

Bynum offered an apology, stating: "When your friends start calling you and repeatedly use the phrase 'I know your heart,' it is a good indicator you've screwed up."

Psychologist Scott Plous suggests the technique used by Bynum's friends is effective because it primes "the speaker's egalitarian self-image," creating a mismatch between who they are and what they did. Plous provides an example: "I'm surprised to hear you say that, because I've always thought of you as someone who is very open-minded." If you're close to the source, try getting more specific: "I've seen how you interact with our customers and know you treat everyone with respect, which is why this recent interaction jumped out at me."

Unless the source is an out-and-out bigot, there's a good chance they're already feeling judged or beating themselves up for their mistake. As we discussed in Principle 2 (Build Resilience), people tend to blow feedback out of proportion, which in turn can provoke outsized fear, anger, guilt, or hopelessness. Failing to separate the behavior from the person will only amplify whatever negative emotion they're already feeling.

## Show You're Learning Too

Social psychologist Dolly Chugh sometimes gives a guest lecture at the course we designed on leadership, diversity, and inclusion, which we've taught with each other and with our colleague Jessica Moldovan. In one class visit, Chugh began her presentation by sharing a story about a professor who'd made a slew of mistakes on identity issues. The professor had mispronounced students' names repeatedly throughout the semester, despite being publicly corrected; confused some students who belonged to the same social identity with each other; called on men more than on women;

interrupted women more than men; filled the syllabus with examples overwhelmingly dominated by white male protagonists; and assigned a reading with a sexist example.

Chugh then revealed she was the professor in question. A whoosh of relief swept over the room. It was hugely reassuring to know that even Chugh—one of the most inclusive scholars and human beings we know—could make these mistakes. In offering this self-disclosure, Chugh was following her advice to "make your own growth visible." She observes that this strategy helps create what leadership and management scholar Amy Edmondson calls "psychological safety"—a climate in which people feel able to make mistakes without being humiliated or punished.

We try to adopt the same approach in our work. Our own lapses over the years include confusing students of the same race with each other; not noticing a syllabus was overpopulated with white male scholars; forgetting to make documents and events fully accessible to people with disabilities; misgendering people; laughing at objectionable jokes; sharing our own allyship practices with an expectation of receiving cookies; and failing to confront non-inclusive behavior. Whenever we share such mistakes, we also notice shoulders relax and arms uncross in the room. Audiences become more open to learning about their own diversity and inclusion errors when we signal we're all on the journey together. They realize that we won't shame them not only for *who* they are, but also for *where* they are in the learning process.

Sharing your own learning interrupts an unfortunate dynamic that can arise when an ally confronts a source. By definition, allies distinguish themselves from others by acting virtuously. In an article titled "Holier Than Me?" social psychologist Benoît Monin points out that when people compare themselves to such moral paragons, they have a choice. They can admire them and seek to emulate them, or they can resent them and seek to take them down a peg.

In making that choice, they're guided by whether they feel judged by the paragons. One of Monin's studies looked at how meat-eaters view vegetarians. When omnivorous participants were asked to rate vegetarians on a series of traits, their ratings were more negative when they were first asked to reflect on how vegetarians would see them. They expected vegetarians to judge them negatively, so they beat them to it.

In another Monin study, researchers asked participants to complete a "police decision task." The participants looked at photographs and descriptions of three burglary suspects with instructions to find the culprit. Two of the suspects were white and one was Black. The researchers deliberately designed the task to incriminate the Black suspect by ensuring he had a criminal record, had no job or alibi, and had cash and a weapon when apprehended. Predictably, the vast majority of participants selected the Black suspect as the likely burglar.

As you've probably guessed, the study wasn't about the detective skills of the participants. The researchers also asked the participants to judge the personality of someone else who'd completed the same survey. Unbeknownst to the participants, this person was a creation of the researchers. The fake response read: "I refuse to make a choice here—this task is obviously biased. . . . Offensive to make black man the obvious suspect. I refuse to play this game."

How did the participants feel about this conscientious objector? The answer depended on whether they completed their own response before or after reading the ally's response. Those who read the ally's response beforehand thought the ally was "strong," "independent," and "socially conscious" for refusing to play the game. Those who had already selected the Black suspect as guilty felt the ally was "self-righteous," "opinionated," and "easily offended."

This knee-jerk response to the virtuous—known as "do-gooder derogation"—is a risk when you're an ally to the source of non-inclusive behavior, because your actions seem to position you as morally superior. Happily, Monin's studies also suggest a strategy for overcoming this problem: don't make the source feel they're being judged and found wanting.

Showing your own learning will help the source feel less judged. The other person is much more likely to hear you and accept your feedback if they perceive you as a flawed peer than if they perceive you as a smug do-gooder. Imagine you're sitting in the break room at your workplace fretting about a mistake. A colleague comes up to you and says, "Yikes—what you did there was pretty sexist. You might want to unlearn the biased assumptions that caused you to behave that way." Now imagine a different colleague approaches you and says, "I think what you did had a negative impact on Esther, but last month I did something similar and here's how I recovered. . . . Next month I'm sure I'll mess up again, and when that happens I hope you'll come to me as well." The "do-gooder derogation" studies suggest you're more likely to listen to the second colleague. If that's right, then try to show you're learning too when you next confront a source.

## Have Some Responses at the Ready

In a study about homophobia and biphobia, participants widely agreed it was important to confront bias, but told the researchers they didn't know how to do it effectively. One participant, Nicole, said, "Sometimes I've been in a conversation where it's like, 'Oh, this is a good opportunity.'" Yet she'd struggle to find the right words and miss the moment, thinking, *Shoot! I blew it. I should have said something.* Due to this lack of confidence, the researchers found participants would "often fail to confront even in situations in which they want to."

Even if you've absorbed our advice to "separate the behavior from the person" and "show you're learning too," you might still wonder, like Nicole, what precise words should come out of your mouth. We generally don't like to provide scripts, because they turn nuanced human interactions into wooden performances. But we bend that rule here because these situations raise special concerns. Confronting a source typically feels adversarial; it frequently also needs to occur in the moment. For these reasons, allies often freeze. They experience "escalator wit," where they think of the right words only after the moment has passed.

To help you engage sources of non-inclusive behavior more confidently, we lay out a menu of options—some from our own work and some from the work of others.

| STRATEGY | EXAMPLES |
|---|---|
| **Say something short and sharp** | "Excuse me?" |
| | "Ouch!" |
| **Emphasize the impact on you** | "That comment didn't land well on me, because . . ." |
| | "I felt uncomfortable about what you just said, because . . ." |
| **Show how your views have evolved** | "I've been [reading / listening to] __ recently and here's how it changed my mind. . . ." |
| | "I used to agree with your perspective, but I was convinced of __ when . . ." |
| **Affirm their values** | "I know you care about __. What you just said doesn't sound consistent with that." |

| STRATEGY | EXAMPLES |
|---|---|
| | "I think you're so much better than that comment." |
| **Affirm their intentions** | "I know you intended that as a joke, but I found it off-putting, because . . ." |
| | "While I'm sure you didn't mean it to come across this way, I found that insulting." |
| **Connect the issue to specific people** | "I have a friend who belongs to that community. My experience with her is different from what you describe." |
| | "If someone said that to your spouse, how would you feel?" |
| **Appeal to organizational values** | "We don't do that kind of thing here." |
| | "As the team leader, it's my responsibility to uphold an inclusive culture, so I need to address what you just said. . . ." |
| **Educate** | "I feel differently about that issue. Can I share my perspective?" |
| | "I just read a great article on this topic. Could I send it your way?" |
| **Model what they could have said** | "I think the client would really like *her*" (in response to misgendering) |
| | "She's incredibly sharp, period" (in response to the comment: "She's incredibly sharp for her age") |
| **Ask them to explain their views** | "Can you help me understand how you came to that view?" |
| | "I didn't get that joke. Could you explain it to me?" |
| **Paraphrase or repeat what they said** | "To make sure I heard you correctly, did you just say __?" |
| | "So, you're suggesting __, is that right?" |

This menu is obviously not complete. Instead, it's meant to give you options so you can choose the ones most authentic to you. We're both analytical and nonconfrontational, which leads us to ask questions or share feedback gently. Pithy soundbites like "Ouch!" feel inauthentic to us. One of Kenji's go-to phrases is: "As someone who believes in an inclusive culture, I'd ask you to rethink that comment." One of David's is: "When you said __, I felt __." Neither, of course, is perfect. A student has already told Kenji his line is hopelessly pious. He still likes it because it reminds him to speak up on his own behalf, correcting his tendency to bring affected people into the conversation unnecessarily. And David likes his phrase because it stops him from assuming anything about the source's intent and focuses the conversation on his own emotional reaction. We invite you to experiment to find words that sound most natural to you. Having a couple of go-to phrases can help you make the intervention in the room rather than on the escalator.

## When You Can Opt Out of Allyship to the Source

Early on a spring morning in a section of New York City's Central Park known as the Ramble, a Black male birdwatcher, Christian Cooper, asked a white woman to leash her dog according to the rules of that area. The woman, later identified as Amy Cooper (no relation), refused, leading Christian Cooper to coax her dog toward him with a treat. Amy Cooper then allegedly yelled at him not to touch her dog, and he started recording the incident on his phone.

The video starts with Amy Cooper demanding that Christian Cooper stop filming her. He continues to film, leading her to say she's about to "call the cops." He responds: "Please call the cops." She starts tapping her phone and adds: "I'm going to tell them there's an African American man threatening my life," to which he responds, "Please tell them whatever you like." Next, she puts the phone up to her ear and says: "There's a man, African American, he has a bicycle helmet, he's recording me and threatening me and my dog." After a brief pause, she repeats: "There is an African American man, I am in Central Park, he is recording me and threatening myself and my dog." The recording shows him standing well away from her. At this point, Amy Cooper raises her voice: "I'm sorry, I can't hear you either. I'm being threatened by a man in the Ramble. Please send the cops immediately!" After Christian Cooper's sister posted the video on the internet, it went viral as an example of everyday racism that could have had dire repercussions for him. As a consequence of her behavior, Amy Cooper was fired.

When we urge people to be allies to the source, we routinely get some version of the question: "Do I need to be an ally to Amy Cooper?" Our answer is a resounding no. You certainly can be an ally to her if you wish, but you shouldn't feel obliged to do so. We think your obligation to be an ally is strongest when you have thick bonds to the source, such as when they're part of your family, friendship circle, school, or workplace. When you have these local community ties, it will be more feasible and more effective for you to help the source grow past their mistakes. In contrast, when someone is a stranger to you (as we assume Amy Cooper is), you don't need to go out of your way to offer assistance.

You also don't need to be an ally to the source when they're unreceptive to help. Chugh offers the "20/60/20 rule" based on the work of global change consultant Susan Lucia Annunzio. While granting that the numbers are fuzzy, Chugh says roughly 20 percent of people are the "easy twenty" who are enthusiastic about diversity and inclusion and want to get better. Another 20 percent are the "stuck twenty" who aren't open to change. Perhaps they're fiercely opposed to diversity and inclusion efforts, they've rebuffed previous attempts at allyship, or they've done something egregious like engaging in sexual harassment or expressing overt bigotry. The final category is the "middle sixty," which consists of people who are largely passive in this area and could be pulled in either direction. Chugh observes that, in general, individuals expend too much energy trying to persuade the stuck twenty when they should focus their efforts on the movable middle. If you've ever spent time arguing with people on the internet, you can probably relate.

Be careful before you assign someone to the stuck twenty category, as people can surprise you. Even Megan Phelps-Roper, former spokesperson of the Westboro Baptist Church from *Snyder v. Phelps*, rethought her entire worldview based on "extended, ongoing conversation." She's now an outspoken advocate of inclusion. Yet once you're confident someone is immovable, we agree with Chugh's tough-minded advice. Don't burn time and energy attempting a conversation with someone who has no interest in it.

Finally, you don't need to be an ally to the source if you're engaged in political activism. Sometimes, even when you have the option of rehabilitating a source through conversation, you might have other overriding goals, like trying to create systemic change. When the source is in a position of power—like a government official or a leader of an organization—you might deliberately stoke conflict through tactics like sit-ins, callouts, or walkouts. If you've thought about the reasons to be an ally to the source and decided it's more important to pursue an activist response, we of course respect that decision.

A labor-organizer friend tried to get her university administration to recognize a new union. Even after multiple conversations, the dean in charge of the issue emphatically disagreed with her. As a seasoned activist, she prepared to do battle by organizing a strike. The main obstacle she encountered startled her: her potential supporters in the university adored the dean and didn't want to upset him. "In my decades of activism," she said, "I've never had to deal with fellow activists lying awake at night worrying about whether they're going to make management cry." She ultimately persuaded her colleagues that getting recognition for the union was more important than having civil conversations with the dean.

This brings us back to Ben at the Thanksgiving dinner. As we've noted, we believe Ben should have been an ally to his grandfather Harold. As his family member, Harold forms part of Ben's community. He also isn't in the stuck twenty—according to Melissa, he may need some time to adjust to social change, but he's not bigoted or resistant to growth. Finally, the family gathering wasn't a moment of political activism. A more generous approach would have allowed Harold to learn. It might also have preserved his relationship with Melissa and Paul.

Loretta Ross is a human rights activist and scholar. In a course she teaches at Smith College and in a related TED talk, she urges people to "call in" rather than to "call out"—in our terminology, to be allies to sources of non-inclusive behavior rather than canceling them.

Ross had her own experience at a family gathering similar to the story that opens this chapter. Her relative Frank silenced what had otherwise been a pleasant conversation at the dinner table by making comments about "Mexican Americans stealing jobs." Ross noted that most people in the room "buried their faces in their plate." But she decided to put her calling-in practice to work. She turned to him and said: "Uncle Frank, I know you. I love you. I respect you. And what I know about you is that you'd run into a burning building and save somebody if you could. And you wouldn't care what race that person is, you wouldn't care whether they were gay or an immigrant. So, Uncle Frank, that's the man I love and respect. So tell me: How can I reconcile that good Uncle Frank that I know you are with the words that just came out of your mouth?"

Ross decided to be Frank's ally in that moment. She didn't accuse him of having malicious intentions or suggest he was a bad person. Instead, she affirmed him and primed him to reflect on the mismatch between his identity and his actions. The comment interrupted Frank's bias but, as Ross put it, didn't lead to "hate, argument, and throwing over the table." It just called on Frank to shift from living under his ideals to living up to them. It gave him the grace to grow.

## Principle 7 **TAKEAWAYS**

- When someone engages in non-inclusive behavior, consider whether to be their ally. You don't need to offer allyship when the source is a stranger to you, they're unreceptive to help, or you're engaged in political activism.

- Separate the behavior from the person. Don't assume negative intent from a harmful impact. Affirm the source as a person while you give feedback on their behavior.

- Show you're learning too. Avoid being dismissed as a smug do-gooder by approaching the source as a flawed peer and sharing times when you've made similar mistakes.

- Choose one or two go-to phrases for challenging bias that are authentic to you.

# Conclusion:

## The Essential Conversations

Consider these four real-life conversations:

*A white male leader holds an event with his employees to address racial injustice. He begins by observing that until recently, he'd thought of his life as a bootstraps narrative about someone who rose from a working-class background to lead a large company. He then shares that he's come to see his story as also one about privilege. He says it's hard to imagine he could have achieved the same level of success struggling against the headwinds of racial bias, and pledges to work to eradicate that bias in his industry. He closes by saying he's still learning and will spend most of the session listening. Employees of all racial backgrounds largely appreciate his comments.*

*A woman is out for a walk with her toddler when they come across a man in a wheelchair. The child asks loudly:*

*"Why is he in that chair?!" The mother responds: "Well, maybe his legs need a bit of extra help, just like Grandma's pancreas needs help." The man is relieved the woman didn't treat disability as a taboo topic or shame her child for asking.*

*A college professor has always drawn huge class enrollments because of his charisma and expertise. Nevertheless, some women in his class complain to the administration that he calls women, but not men, terms of endearment like "darling" or "dearest." The administration sends another professor to tell him to stop. Speaking in his office, the colleague says she finds the conversation difficult because everyone, including her, has made mistakes in their interactions with students. Initially, he disagrees with her suggestion that his behavior is inappropriate, claiming he uses diminutives to build warmth and trust. She agrees he's incredibly committed to the well-being of his students, which is why she was surprised to hear he did anything that affected them negatively. He listens carefully to her feedback about the impact of his actions on his women students, stops defending himself, and ultimately changes his behavior.*

*A gay activist takes on a major educational project about trans rights. His work in gay rights has regularly led him to engage in trans advocacy, making him think he's reasonably qualified to speak on these issues. He then misgenders his trans colleague Julia. He apologizes immediately and moves on. He later refers to "sex-change surgery," and she tells him the right term is "gender confir-*

*mation surgery." In reflecting on his missteps, he realizes he doesn't know enough about trans identity to complete the project. Against some resistance from stakeholders, he slows down the timeline to become better informed. He also asks Julia if she'd like to contribute to the project as a paid consultant. She says yes.*

Of course, these conversations could have easily gone in other directions. We could imagine employees of color thinking the corporate leader's decision to spend most of the session listening was a dodge, or the trans colleague thinking she should be leading the project herself rather than being paid to educate a gay activist to do so. Yet while our principles won't guarantee success in all cases, we hope they'll help you navigate past many of the errors we've canvassed in this book.

At the beginning of the book, we pledged to give you practical advice, not to shame you, and to galvanize you to action. Whether we were able to deliver on those three promises is not for us to say—that's for you to decide. In closing, we simply offer our hopes for you with regard to each promise.

First, we hope you'll be practical by practicing. If we've done our job, you might feel a sense of relief that you've filled a chest with the tools you need for identity conversations. But as time goes on, we suspect you'll encounter several challenges putting the principles into practice. Sometimes you won't remember what to do, or you won't execute on a principle properly. In those cases, you can return to this book for a refresher course. At other times, you might realize the issue runs deeper.

You may have noticed that we've outlined a lot of guidelines and exceptions over these pages, and some of them seem maddeningly at odds with each other:

- Listen attentively, but don't withdraw into silence.

- Drive a wedge between intent and impact, but sometimes share intent to soften impact.

- Don't ignore people's group identity, but also don't reduce them to their group identity.

- Be open to apologizing more, but don't over-apologize.

- Seek guidance from affected people when in doubt about what to do, but don't expect them to educate you.

These tensions aren't contradictions, but each requires judgment. We understand why they might cause anxiety, especially since this list is incomplete.

By working through these tensions, we think you'll discover that conversations about identity, as with any genuine human interactions, can never be a box-ticking exercise. As we were writing this book, many people said: "Just tell me what to say and I'll say it!" We can certainly provide suggested language here and there, as you've seen, but we've never been able to write a script for people to read out verbatim. By their nature, identity conversations don't lend themselves to quick fixes. Indeed, the power of conversation is that it can respond to the complexity of human life with subtlety and flexibility. No script, no policy, no rule book can help you manage paradoxes as well as dialogue can.

What we wish for you here is captured in one directive: practice, practice, practice. Getting better at conversations about identity is like learning a new language. You may never reach native-level proficiency, but you'll improve with practice. And practice you will—the next identity conversation is always around the corner. If you adopt a growth mindset, we're confident applying our principles will become second nature.

The second promise we made was that we wouldn't shame you. Plenty of people will. In our experience, they're usually motivated by understandable emotions, such as the feeling that they've tried everything else to no avail, and that only the blunt-edged method remains. They worry a kinder approach will let allies off the hook when the people truly suffering are the targets of non-inclusive behavior.

We've wrestled with the question of how compassionate we can afford to be in coaching allies. At the outset, we told you we see diversity and inclusion issues from the bridge. By temperament, we strive to understand where all sides are coming from and tend to see issues more in gray than in black and white. Yet our perspective on issues of identity, diversity, and justice is far from neutral. We'll always empathize more with the plight of marginalized people than with the fears of the dominant group.

That perspective can make it tempting to approach allies like stern boot-camp instructors, hectoring them for mistakes and telling them they're weak for finding this work difficult or tiring. But we believe that's an unhelpful path. We think compassion and accountability go hand in hand. If you believe a mistake will turn you into a bad person, you'll try to justify your behavior. Yet if you know you can retain your integrity while admitting to errors, your guard will come down. You'll be more likely to say: "You're right. I screwed up and I'm sorry. Thanks for letting me know."

Our hope here is that you don't prove us wrong. We want you to be compassionate to yourself as you grow in this domain. But we hope it doesn't stop there. We're wagering everything on the idea that individuals who extend grace toward themselves are tougher on their own behaviors. We're counting on you to hold yourself accountable.

Our final hope for you has to do with our promise to motivate you to action. While we've believed in the power of conversation for a long time, our primary concern has always been social justice. We want you to take what you've learned and apply it, not to dazzle people with your eloquence but to make a difference in your communities. Speak up at your next school board meeting or local town hall. Plan an event at your workplace. Join an organization that fights for civil rights and use your voice to advance its mission.

At times, you may struggle with the task of being an ally and feel like giving up. If that happens, we hope you keep the importance of what you're doing steadily visible. We both became lawyers because we believed the law was a powerful tool for achieving equal dignity for all. We still believe in the law's power and revere the lawyers who fight for civil rights in legislative chambers and courtrooms. But we believe the work of civil rights is being done just as much in rooms like your classroom, your break room, or your living room. As you enter identity conversations, we want you to think of them as moments when you use your moral agency in the domains in which you have power. This is the work of civil rights only you can do.

So next time you have to decide whether to speak up or not, we hope you remember why you do this turbulent work. You do it to speak from the best part of yourself, so others can do the same. You do it to honor the many valid ways there are to be a human being. And most of all, you do it because you yearn for justice, and are willing to fight for it. We wish you joy in that struggle.

# Acknowledgments

So many people believed in this book and helped us bring it to fruition.

We want to start by thanking the former dean of NYU School of Law, Trevor Morrison, for launching our center and giving us the resources and support needed to be successful in our work. We also want to thank our past and present colleagues and partners of the Meltzer Center for Diversity, Inclusion, and Belonging who have helped us with various aspects of completing this book or have informed our thinking on these issues: Cory Conley, Shirley Dang, Gabriel Delabra, Irene Dorzback, Kathryn Jones, Jessica Moldovan, Adriana Ogle, Schele Williams, and Annmarie Zell. We are incredibly grateful to have such dedicated and insightful collaborators in this work.

Early in the writing process, we convened a reading group for first-year law students on the topic of identity conversations. Thank you to Danielle Altchiler, Eloisa Cleveland, Vico Fortier, David Hamburger, Emily Herzfeld, Eliza Hopkins, Cheng-Hau Kee, Brittany Lee, Daniela Purpuro, Lydia Seifeselassie, Tina Szpicek, and Joanna Wolfgram for being an invaluable sounding board for our ideas.

Two of those students—David Hamburger and Eliza Hopkins—later joined us as student researchers, along with an equally extraordinary group of peers, many of whom worked with us over more than one semester: Eli Ashenafi, Matthew Brehm, Emily Chang, Dnyaneshwari Chincholikar, Gabriel Delabra, Alma Diamond, Dmitry Dobrovolskiy, Zoe Farkas, Sumner Fields, Abhilasha Gokulan, Andrea Green, Myra Hyder, Chihiro Isozaki, Shruti Kannan, Melody Karmana, Erin Kim, Deborah Leffell, Mariana Múnera, Sakiko Nishida, Daniel Putnam, Brittany Shaar, Wenny Shen, Zoë Smith, Eva Vivero, Hadiya Williams, and Mikayla Wilson. Each one of these students sharpened our ideas, pointed us to unfamiliar research, and offered incisive critiques of draft chapters. We were privileged to learn from them all.

We thank all the early readers who took substantial time out of their busy schedules to provide comments on a draft of the manuscript: Kim Chaloner, Jyoti Chopra, Dolly Chugh, Shari Coats, Steve Coats, Abby Freireich, Roy Germano, Andrew Glasgow, Kim Glasgow, Milana Hogan, Lindsay Kendrick, Kyra Laursen, Betsy Lerner, Gary Lo, George Loening, Lindsay-Rae McIntyre, Brett Millar, Clive Mullett, Julie Nestingen, Renée Noel, Bethany Davis Noll, Erin O'Brien, Lourdes Olvera-Marshall, Michèle Penzer, Vincent Southerland, Donna Stoneham, Ron Stoneham, George Walker, Mark Weinsier, Lara Werbeloff, and Andy Williams. Their feedback made this book immeasurably better.

We are eternally grateful to our agent, Betsy Lerner, who spent months coaching us to write the best book proposal we could muster and found us a home at Atria. Betsy has served as a trusted advisor throughout this process and has gone above and beyond her role as an agent by providing substantive feedback on the book manuscript. We couldn't ask for a better advocate.

Stephanie Hitchcock, our editor at Atria, richly deserves her stellar reputation. From the outset, she offered wise counsel on tone, structure, and storytelling, and always urged us to keep the book's purpose steadily visible—greater inclusion and belonging for people who are excluded and marginalized. We are thankful for her moral clarity and editorial guidance. We also want to thank the whole sterling team at Atria, including copyediting, art, publicity, sales and marketing, and editorial assistants Alejandra Rocha and Erica Siudzinski.

We would also like to thank our terrific publicist, Angela Baggetta. Angela is everything we could have hoped for in a publicist: wise, responsive, and kind. As soon as we met her, we knew she was the partner we needed to get this book its widest possible audience. We are lucky to have had the opportunity to work with her.

We are indebted to Roger Meltzer, chairman emeritus of DLA Piper and trustee of NYU School of Law, after whom our research center is named. Roger has been the center's biggest champion. He is a true believer in our mission of creating more inclusive institutions and societies. We've had the time and resources to develop our ideas and pursue our work on identity conversations thanks in large part to his unflagging support.

## Additional Acknowledgments from Kenji

My first round of thanks goes to my coauthor, David Glasgow. I have historically been leery of coauthoring work, but this collaboration has been a joy. Your compassion, intelligence, and work ethic are more unique than rare.

I also want to thank the Filomen D'Agostino and Max E. Greenberg Faculty Research Fund of NYU School of Law for research support.

I would like to thank my parents, Michael and Chiyoko Yoshino, who modeled resilience throughout the pandemic, as they have throughout their lives. You were my first role models, and continue to serve as such.

I would like to thank my children, Sophia and Luke, for the unmitigated joy they bring into my life. I knew from the outset that you would be the great gifts of my life. I am grateful for you every day.

I want to thank our family's personal assistant, Marcia Longman, for making sure the ships sail on time.

Our Great Dane, Lucy, always instinctively knows when any family member needs some comfort, and spent many hours at my feet as I worked on this manuscript. I hope the same instinct teaches her how much she means to us all.

Finally, this is the third book in which I get to reserve my deepest thanks for my husband, Ron. Every year we spend together allows me to say with greater confidence that I have never met a finer human being.

## Additional Acknowledgments from David

I want to start by thanking my coauthor, Kenji. Your knowledge, experience, generosity, and sense of humor made writing this book truly enjoyable. I couldn't imagine a better partner in this work.

I am grateful for the steadfast support offered by my parents, Kim Glasgow and Clive Mullett. They imparted values of diversity, inclusion, and belonging to me from a young age, and have always encouraged me in my academic and professional pursuits. I am lucky to be their son.

My two children, Hugo and Theodore, keep reminding me what matters most. Regardless of how tired or stressed I get, their faces never cease to make me smile. Thank you for your playfulness, your curiosity, and your cuddles on the sofa. Even as toddlers, you always look out for other people's feelings and display compassion and kindness toward all living beings. I know you will grow up to make the world a more inclusive place.

Thank you to Chloé White, my kids' nanny throughout most of the writing process. Caregivers are indispensable to the professional success of working parents, yet are all too often invisible and underappreciated. Thank you for the love, attention, and kindness you show my children day after day.

Finally, I thank my husband and favorite conversation partner, Andrew Glasgow. No words can possibly capture my endless gratitude. We embarked on this project at a challenging time— during a pandemic with an infant and a toddler. Throughout all the stress of recent years, you have supported and encouraged me every step of the way. You've taken on extra childcare responsibilities, listened to all my anxieties and fears and hopes, and provided input into every aspect of this book. I am extremely fortunate to be married to such a kind and generous person. I love you.

# Notes

**Introduction: The Impossible Conversations**

4   *What's new about the present* Jennifer Richeson, "The Psychology Behind a Divided America," *Innovation Lab* podcast, February 13, 2018, 22:59 at 20:12, https://soundcloud.com/innovationhub /the-psychology-behind-a-divided-america.

5   *As speechwriter Jon Favreau* Jon Favreau, "Chimamanda Ngozi Adichie Talks Her Viral Essay and Vitriol on Social Media | Offline Podcast," *Crooked Media*, January 16, 2022, YouTube video, 56:59 at 16:42, https://www.youtube.com/watch?v=urOJKvCy79Q.

5   *Journalist Emily Yoffe mourns* Emily Yoffe, *Intent Matters—The Good Fight with Yascha Mounk (Emily Yoffe),* March 8, 2021, YouTube video, 1:07:05 at 3:37, https://www.youtube.com/watch?v=Rp0SuhEOiI0.

5   *Political scientist Yascha Mounk* Yascha Mounk, *Intent Matters— The Good Fight with Yascha Mounk (Emily Yoffe),* March 8, 2021, YouTube video, 1:07:05 at 4:24.

5   *The* New York Times *profiled* Amy Harmon, "BIPOC or POC? Equity or Equality? The Debate Over Language on the Left," *New York Times*, November 1, 2021, https://www.nytimes.com/2021/11/01 /us/terminology-language-politics.html.

6   *In the United States* Jeffrey Jones, "U.S. Church Membership Falls Below Majority for First Time," Gallup, March 29, 2021, https://news .gallup.com/poll/341963/church-membership-falls-below-majority

-first-time.aspx; "In U.S., Decline of Christianity Continues at Rapid Pace," Pew Research Center, October 17, 2019, https://www.pewforum .org/2019/10/17/in-u-s-decline-of-christianity-continues-at-rapid -pace/; Dudley Poston and Rogelio Sáenz, "Demographic Trends Spell the End of the White Majority in 2044," AP News, May 25, 2019, https://apnews.com/article/4a60c86e938045fa80dad97f67ce9120; Noor Wazwaz, "It's Official: The U.S. Is Becoming a Minority-Majority Nation," *U.S. News*, July 6, 2015, https://www.usnews.com /news/articles/2015/07/06/its-official-the-us-is-becoming-a -minority-majority-nation; Carter Sherman, "Gen Z Says It's America's Queerest Generation Yet," *Vice*, February 24, 2021, https://www.vice .com/en/article/m7an8a/gen-z-says-its-americas-queerest -generation-yet; Jeffrey Jones, "LGBT Identification Rises to 5.6% in Latest U.S. Estimate," Gallup, February 24, 2021, https://news.gallup .com/poll/329708/lgbt-identification-rises-latest-estimate.aspx.

6    *Andy Dunn, an entrepreneur* Emma Goldberg, "The 37-Year-Olds Are Afraid of the 23-Year-Olds Who Work for Them," *New York Times*, October 28, 2021, https://www.nytimes.com/2021/10/28 /business/gen-z-workplace-culture.html.

7    *As Gloria Steinem once* Gloria Steinem, "The Progression of Feminism: Where Are We Going," *C-Span Talk*, March 26, 2007, 1:14:52 at 13:37, https://www.c-span.org/video/?197336-1/progression-feminism.

7    *Some daycare centers even* Alia Wong, "Kids Develop Views on Race When They're Young. Here's How Some Preschools Are Responding," *USA Today*, September 23, 2021, https://www.usatoday.com /story/news/education/2021/09/23/race-theory-preschool-how -to-teach-kids-about-racism/5796892001/; "Diversity, Equity, and Inclusion at KinderCare," KinderCare, accessed January 13, 2022, https://www.kindercare.com/resources/diversity-equity-inclusion.

8    *An article in the* Economist "Diversity Fatigue," *Economist*, February 13, 2016, https://www.economist.com/business/2016/02/11 /diversity-fatigue (edited to conform to American spelling); Joanne Lipman, *That's What She Said: What Men and Women Need to Know About Working Together* (New York: William Morrow, 2018), 68–88.

8    *As the former diversity director* Chris Weller, "Apple's VP of Diversity Says '12 White, Blue-eyed, Blonde Men in a Room' Can Be a Diverse Group," *Insider*, October 11, 2017, https://www.businessinsider.com /apples-vp-diversity-12-white-men-can-be-diverse-group-2017-10.

8    *At other times, leaders stoke* Tema Okun, "White Supremacy Culture,"

accessed January 13, 2022, https://cdn.ymaws.com/www.wpha.org
/resource/resmgr/health_&_racial_equity/whitesupremacyculture
inorgan.pdf.

9    *We suspended judgment* Julie L. Earles, Laura L. Vernon, and Jeanne
     P. Yetz, "Equine-Assisted Therapy for Anxiety and Posttraumatic
     Stress Symptoms," *Journal of Traumatic Stress* 28, no. 2 (April 2015):
     149, https://doi.org/10.1002/jts.21990; Sudha M. Srinivasan, David
     T. Cavagnino, and Anjana N. Bhat, "Effects of Equine Therapy on
     Individuals with Autism Spectrum Disorder: A Systematic Review,"
     *Review Journal of Autism and Developmental Disorders* 5 (June
     2018): 156, https://doi.org/10.1007/s40489-018-0130-z.

12   *In the medical profession* Eileen E. Morrison, *Ethics in Health
     Administration: A Practical Approach for Decision-Makers*, 4th ed.
     (Burlington, MA: Jones and Bartlett Learning, 2020), chap. 3.

## Principle 1: Beware the Four Conversational Traps

16   *Some experts on conversations* Robin DiAngelo, *White Fragility:
     Why It's So Hard for White People to Talk About Racism* (Bos-
     ton: Beacon Press, 2018), 9; Reni Eddo-Lodge, *Why I'm No Longer
     Talking to White People About Race* (New York: Bloomsbury Pub-
     lishing, 2017), 91.

16   *Former Fox News host* Eric Bolling, "Eric Bolling Walks Off During
     Heated Live BBC Debate on Georgia Election Law," Vicmar Arquiza,
     April 8, 2021, YouTube video, 6:48, https://www.youtube.com/watch
     ?v=MiDhQmwuyM8.

17   *A nondisabled man told* Diane J. Goodman, *Promoting Diversity
     and Social Justice: Educating People from Privileged Groups* (New
     York: Routledge, 2011), 89.

18   *Writer Savala Nolan argues* Christina Capatides, "White Silence on
     Social Media: Why Not Saying Anything Is Actually Saying a Lot,"
     CBS News, June 3, 2020, https://www.cbsnews.com/news/white
     -silence-on-social-media-why-not-saying-anything-is-actually-saying
     -a-lot/.

18   *During recent spikes in antisemitism* Melissa Block and Jerome
     Socolovsky, "Antisemitism Spikes, and Many Jews Wonder: Where
     Are Our Allies?," NPR, June 7, 2021, https://www.npr.org/2021/06
     /07/1003411933/antisemitism-spikes-and-many-jews-wonder-where
     -are-our-allies.

18    *"I am saddened and appalled"* Alexandra Tsuneta, "Your Silence
      About Antisemitism Is Deafening," *An Injustice!*, May 27, 2021,
      https://aninjusticemag.com/your-silence-about-anti-semitism
      -is-deafening-41bd4e41ffef (accessed January 24, 2022; site inactive
      on October 19, 2022).

18    *He recognized that* Robin J. Ely and David A. Thomas, "Getting
      Serious About Diversity: Enough Already with the Business Case,"
      *Harvard Business Review*, November–December 2020, https:
      //hbr.org/2020/11/getting-serious-about-diversity-enough-already
      -with-the-business-case.

19    *As disability activist Carly Findlay* Carly Findlay, "This Is How It
      Feels When You Say 'I Don't See Your Disability,'" *Carly Findlay*
      (blog), July 18, 2016, https://carlyfindlay.com.au/2016/07/18/this-is
      -how-it-feels-when-you-say-i-dont-see-your-disability/.

19    *According to writer Melissa Fabello* Melissa A. Fabello, "4 Things
      Men Are Really Doing When They 'Play Devil's Advocate' Against
      Feminism," *Everyday Feminism*, September 6, 2015, https://
      everydayfeminism.com/2015/09/playing-devils-advocate/.

21    *Writer Layla Saad says* Layla F. Saad, *Me and White Supremacy:
      Combat Racism, Change the World, and Become a Good Ancestor*
      (Naperville, IL: Sourcebooks, 2020), 51.

22    *He killed eight individuals* Hanna Park, "He Shot at 'Everyone He
      Saw': Atlanta Spa Workers Recount Horrors of Shooting," NBC
      News, April 2, 2021, https://www.nbcnews.com/news/asian-america
      /he-shot-everyone-he-saw-atlanta-spa-workers-recount-horrors
      -n1262928.

22    *Media coverage focused on* Roslyn Talusan, "Blaming the Atlanta
      Shooting on 'Temptation' Glosses Over Its Racism," *Vice Magazine*,
      March 23, 2021, https://www.vice.com/en/article/xgzndw/blaming
      -the-atlanta-shooting-on-temptation-glosses-over-its-racism;
      Jiayang Fan, "The Atlanta Shooting and the Dehumanizing of Asian
      Women," *New Yorker*, March 19, 2021, https://www.newyorker.com
      /news/daily-comment/the-atlanta-shooting-and-the-dehumanizing
      -of-asian-women.

22    *It compared the anti-Asian hatred* Marc Ramirez, "Stop Asian
      Hate, Stop Black Hate, Stop All Hate: Many Americans Call for
      Unity Against Racism," *USA Today*, March 20, 2021, https://www
      .usatoday.com/story/news/nation/2021/03/20/atlanta-shootings
      -see-asian-black-americans-take-white-supremacy/4769268001/;

Seren Morris, "Should We Say 'Asian Lives Matter'? Atlanta Shootings Spark Debate," *Newsweek*, March 17, 2021, https://www .newsweek.com/should-we-say-asian-lives-matter-atlanta-shootings -spark-debate-1576764.

22  *A term coined by* Kimberlé Crenshaw, "Demarginalizing the Intersection of Race and Sex: A Black Feminist Critique of Antidiscrimination Doctrine, Feminist Theory, and Antiracist Policies," *University of Chicago Legal Forum* 1, no. 8 (1989): 139–67.

23  *Nancy's insistence on shifting focus* DiAngelo, *White Fragility*, 135.

23  *The interviewer, Ed Livingston* Ed Livingston and Mitch Katz, "Structural Racism for Doctors—What Is It?," *JAMA Podcast*, February 23, 2021, https://canvas.emory.edu/courses/86982/pages /jama-podcast-transcript.

24  *Yet many kindred phrases* For a lengthier discussion of this form of deflection, see Nancy Leong, *Identity Capitalists: The Powerful Insiders Who Exploit Diversity to Maintain Inequality* (Stanford: Stanford University Press, 2021).

25  *In an ingenious study* L. Taylor Phillips and Brian S. Lowery, "The Hard-Knock Life? Whites Claim Hardships in Response to Racial Inequity," *Journal of Experimental Social Psychology* 61 (November 2015): 12–19, https://doi.org/10.1016/j.jesp.2015.06.008.

25  *This "hard-knock life effect"* L. Taylor Phillips and Brian S. Lowery, "I Ain't No Fortunate One: On the Motivated Denial of Class Privilege," *Journal of Personality and Social Psychology* 119, no. 6 (December 2020): 1403–22, https://doi.org/10.1037/pspi0000240.

26  *In response to Donald Trump's stance* Kelly Osbourne, "The View— Kelly Osborne [sic] 'Who is going to be cleaning your toilet, Donald Trump?,'" Francisco The Mage, YouTube video, August 5, 2015, 0:58, https://www.youtube.com/watch?v=NJC_MNjw4E0.

26  *To meet the participants* Tonja Jacobi and Dylan Schweers, "Justice, Interrupted: The Effect of Gender, Ideology, and Seniority at Supreme Court Oral Arguments," *Virginia Law Review* 103 (2017): 1379–496.

26  *According to the study* Ibid., 1466.

27  *In a notable example* Valerie Loftus, "Megyn Kelly Says It's a 'Verifiable Fact' That Santa Is White," *Business Insider*, December 12, 2013, https://www.businessinsider.com/fox-news-santa-is-white -2013-12.

27  *It was also strange because* Jose Delreal, "Scholar: Santa Race Claim

Nonsense," *Politico*, December 13, 2013, https://www.politico.com /story/2013/12/santa-claus-race-claim-megyn-kelly-101152.

28  *In others, he compared* THR Staff, "Trevor Noah Criticized as Anti-Semitic Due to Twitter History," *Hollywood Reporter*, March 31, 2015, https://www.hollywoodreporter.com/tv/tv-news /trevor-noah-criticized-as-anti-785447/; Lauren Gambino, "Daily Show's Trevor Noah Under Fire for Twitter Jokes About Jews and Women," *Guardian*, March 31, 2015, https://www.theguardian .com/culture/2015/mar/31/trevor-noah-backlash-highlights-jokes -jews-women.

28  *Rising to Noah's defense* Jim Norton, "Jim Norton: Trevor Noah Isn't the Problem. You Are," *Time*, April 1, 2015, https://time.com /3766915/trevor-noah-tweets-outrage/.

28  *Noah appeared to take* Lisa de Moraes, "Trevor Noah Dismisses Controversial Tweets as Jokes That 'Didn't Land'—Update," *Deadline*, March 31, 2015, https://deadline.com/2015/03/trevor-noah -controversy-twitter-comedy-central-1201402001/.

28  *Groening was nonchalant* Bill Keveney, " 'The Simpsons' Exclusive: Matt Groening (Mostly) Remembers the Show's Record 636 Episodes," *USA Today*, April 27, 2018, https://www.usatoday .com/story/life/tv/2018/04/27/thesimpsons-matt-groening-new -record-fox-animated-series/524581002/.

28  *When asked for an explanation* Michael Blackmon, "Kevin Hart Is Deleting Old Anti-Gay Tweets After Being Announced as Oscars Host," *BuzzFeed News*, December 6, 2018, https://www.buzzfeednews .com/article/michaelblackmon/kevin-hart-homophobic-tweets-gay -oscars.

30  *As she left the conversation* Jared Richards, "Sia Is Fighting with Fans on Twitter over Casting Maddie Ziegler as Autistic Teen in New Film," *Junkee*, November 23, 2020, https://junkee.com/sia-music -autism-criticism/279474; Chris Willman, "Sia Engages in Fiery Twitter Debate with Disability Activists over Autism-Themed Film," *Variety*, November 20, 2020, https://variety.com/2020/music /news/sia-debate-twitter-disabled-film-autism-music-1234837013/; Rachelle Hampton, "Why Is Sia Cursing Out Autistic Critics on Twitter?," *Slate*, November 20, 2020, https://slate.com/culture /2020/11/sia-autism-twitter-controversy-music-movie-album.html.

30  *Writer Ijeoma Oluo endured* Ijeoma Oluo, *So You Want to Talk About Race* (New York: Seal Press, 2019), 214.

30    *Actor Laurence Fox* Laurence Fox, "Row Breaks Out Over Harry &
      Meghan Royal Finances Question!," BBC, January 17, 2020,
      YouTube video, 13:00, https://www.youtube.com/watch?v=re7K2S
      GMmHU.

30    *A biracial woman* Kayleigh Dray, "Meghan Markle Receives Front
      Page Apology from the Mail on Sunday, Here's a History of the Sh*t
      She's Taken from the British Press and Public," *Stylist*, December
      27, 2021, https://www.stylist.co.uk/people/meghan-markle-racist
      -bullying-tabloids-prince-harry-wardrobe-malfunction-duchess
      -difficult-examples/342213.

31    *Many analysts saw* Ellie Hall, "Here Are 20 Headlines Comparing
      Meghan Markle to Kate Middleton That May Show Why She and
      Prince Harry Left Royal Life," *BuzzFeed*, January 13, 2020, https://
      www.buzzfeednews.com/article/ellievhall/meghan-markle-kate
      -middleton-double-standards-royal; Maya Goodfellow, "Yes, the
      UK Media's Coverage of Meghan Markle Really Is Racist," *Vox*,
      January 17, 2020, https://www.vox.com/first-person/2020/1/17
      /21070351/meghan-markle-prince-harry-leaving-royal-family-uk
      -racism.

32    *That frustration would intensify* For more on the accumulated
      impact of seemingly small behaviors, sometimes known as "mi-
      croaggressions," see Derald Wing Sue and Lisa Beth Spanierman,
      *Microaggressions in Everyday Life*, 2nd ed. (Hoboken: John Wiley &
      Sons, 2020).

## Principle 2: Build Resilience

37    *He and Lipman spent* Joanne Lipman, *That's What She Said: What
      Men and Women Need to Know About Working Together* (New
      York: William Morrow, 2018), x.

38    *The children's book* Angela DiTerlizzi, *The Magical Yet* (New York:
      Little, Brown & Company, 2020).

38    The Magical Yet *tracks psychologist* Carol Dweck, *Mindset: The New
      Psychology of Success* (New York: Ballantine Books, 2007).

39    *She explains that people* Dolly Chugh, *The Person You Mean to
      Be: How Good People Fight Bias* (New York: HarperCollins, 2018),
      23–35.

39    *As Chugh argues* Ibid., 7–9.

39    *In a series of experiments* Priyanka B. Carr et al., " 'Prejudiced'

Behavior Without Prejudice? Beliefs About the Malleability of Prejudice Affect Interracial Interactions," *Journal of Personality and Social Psychology* 103, no. 3 (September 2012): 452–71, https://doi.org/10.1037/a0028849.

40  *They didn't think they could* Dweck, *Mindset*, 36.

40  *When you slip into* "10 Strategies for Talking to Students About Growth Mindsets," The Education Hub, accessed January 14, 2022, https://theeducationhub.org.nz/wp-content/uploads/2018/06/10-strategies-for-talking-to-students-about-growth-mindsets.pdf.

41  *Whenever she made an error* Chai Feldblum, "Seizing the #MeToo Moment: Converting Awareness into Action," NYU School of Law, September 24, 2018, YouTube video, 1:01:31 at 57:10, https://www.youtube.com/watch?v=UHUk9Xx0fVU.

42  *Self-affirmation has been used* Geoffrey L. Cohen and David K. Sherman, "The Psychology of Change: Self-Affirmation and Social Psychological Intervention," *Annual Review of Psychology* 65 (January 2014): 333, 343, 347, 352–53, https://doi.org/10.1146/annurev-psych-010213-115137.

42  *They can "deal with"* Ibid., 338–39.

43  *When you know* Robert Livingston, *The Conversation: How Seeking and Speaking the Truth About Racism Can Radically Transform Individuals and Organizations* (New York: Currency Press, 2021), 231.

43  *As he notes* Ibid., 229.

44  *This means "finding ways"* Douglas Stone and Sheila Heen, *Thanks for the Feedback: The Science and Art of Receiving Feedback Well* (New York: Viking, 2014), 165.

44  *As journalist Reni Eddo-Lodge* Reni Eddo-Lodge, *Why I'm No Longer Talking to White People About Race* (New York: Bloomsbury Publishing, 2017), 87.

44  *When Jennifer Gates* Britney Grover, "Jenn Gates: Learning from Life, Riding, and Medical School," *Sidelines Magazine,* July 17, 2020, https://sidelinesmagazine.com/sidelines-feature/jenn-gates-learning-from-life-riding-and-medical-school.html.

44  *Conservative writer Matt Walsh* Matt Walsh (@MattWalshBlog), "Consider a white child living in a trailer in Clay County, Kentucky. He lives in one of the poorest parts of the country, with perhaps the worst quality of life, and one of the highest suicide, overdose, and drop-out rates. Where does 'white privilege' come into play for

him?," Twitter, June 19, 2020, https://twitter.com/mattwalshblog
/status/1273959513184501760.

45    *He chastised them* Tal Fortgang, "Why I'll Never Apologize for My
White Male Privilege," *Time*, May 2, 2014, https://time.com/85933
/why-ill-never-apologize-for-my-white-male-privilege/.

46    *Some writers and scholars* See, e.g., Vernā A. Myers, *What If I Say
the Wrong Thing? 25 Habits for Culturally Effective People* (Chicago:
American Bar Association, 2013), 41; Debby Irving, *Waking Up White,
and Finding Myself in the Story of Race* (Cambridge, MA: Elephant
Room Press, 2014), 54–60; Chugh, *The Person You Mean to Be*, 62–66.

46    *Journalist Celeste Headlee* Celeste Headlee, *Speaking of Race: Why
Everybody Needs to Talk About Racism—and How to Do It* (New
York: Harper Wave, 2021), 31.

46    *As United States Senator John Kennedy* Josephine Harvey, "GOP
Senator Skewered for Griping About How Much It Hurts to Be Called
a Racist," *HuffPost*, October 12, 2020, https://www.huffpost.com/entry
/john-kennedy-racist-comment_n_5f84cfb7c5b6e5c320026ab2.

47    *"If someone suggests that"* Headlee, *Speaking of Race*, 1.

47    *Here's Ijeoma Oluo* Ijeoma Oluo, *So You Want to Talk About Race*
(New York: Seal Press, 2019), 216–17.

47    *It would be a miracle* "Interview with Beverly Daniel Tatum," PBS,
2003, https://www.pbs.org/race/000_About/002_04-background
-03-04.htm.

48    *Sometimes in these conversations* Lily Zheng, "Enough with the
Corporate Non-Apologies for DEI-Related Harm," *Harvard Business
Review*, April 15, 2022, https://hbr.org/2022/04/enough-with-
the-corporate-non-apologies-for-dei-related-harm.

49    *Merely identifying the difficult emotions* Jared B. Torre and Matthew D. Lieberman, "Putting Feelings into Words: Affect Labeling
as Implicit Emotion Regulation," *Emotion Review* 10, no. 2 (April
2018): 116–24, https://doi.org/10.1177/1754073917742706.

49    *For whatever reason* Marc Schoen, *Your Survival Instinct Is Killing
You* (New York: Plume, 2013), 172.

50    *In a study of university students* Andrew J. Vonasch et al., "Death
Before Dishonor: Incurring Costs to Protect Moral Reputation,"
*Social Psychological and Personality Science* 9, no. 5 (July 2018):
604–13, https://doi.org/10.1177/1948550617720271.

50    *One parent spoke anonymously* Dana Kennedy, "Fed-Up Parents
Plan to Troll Elite NYC Schools with Anti-Woke Billboards," *New*

*York Post*, June 5, 2021, https://nypost.com/2021/06/05/parents
-plan-to-troll-elite-nyc-schools-with-anti-woke-billboards/.

50   *She cites a survey* Lipman, *That's What She Said*, xv.

51   *Judy Morelock, a white college lecturer* Hayes Hickman, "Fired University of Tennessee Lecturer Now Charged with Assault Against
Student," *Knoxville News*, September 29, 2017, https://www.knoxnews
.com/story/news/crime/2017/09/29/fired-ut-lecturer-now-charged
-assault-against-student/715756001/; Renee Parker, "Beware of
Wolves in Sheep's Clothing: The Tale of a Progressive Professor Who
Forgot to Hide Her Racism and Got Her Ass Fired," *Student Voices*,
June 6, 2017, https://mystudentvoices.com/beware-of-wolves-in
-sheeps-clothing-the-tāle-of-a-progressive-professor-who-forgot-to
-hide-her-7efe21b1fc5d.

51   *Diversity expert Verna Myers* Myers, *What If I Say the Wrong
Thing?*, 53–54.

52   *Psychologist Kristin Neff gives* Kristin Neff, *Self-Compassion: The
Proven Power of Being Kind to Yourself* (New York: William Morrow, 2011), 91.

52   *If you don't stop* Ibid.

54   *The colleague responded* Susan Silk and Barry Goldman, "How Not
to Say the Wrong Thing," *Los Angeles Times*, April 7, 2013, https://
www.latimes.com/opinion/op-ed/la-xpm-2013-apr-07-la-oe-0407
-silk-ring-theory-20130407-story.html.

56   *As Arab Australian writer* Ruby Hamad, "How White Women Use
Strategic Tears to Silence Women of Colour," *Guardian*, May 7,
2018, https://www.theguardian.com/commentisfree/2018/may/08
/how-white-women-use-strategic-tears-to-avoid-accountability
(edited to conform to American spelling).

56   *Author Adiba Jaigirdar* Adiba Jaigirdar, "The Unsafe Space," in
*Allies: Real Talk About Showing Up, Screwing Up, and Trying Again*,
ed. Shakirah Bourne and Dana Alison Levy (New York: DK Publishing, 2021), 120–29.

57   *Library assistant Jennifer Loubriel* Jennifer Loubriel, "4 Ways
White People Can Process Their Emotions Without Bringing the
White Tears," *Everyday Feminism*, February 16, 2016, https://
everydayfeminism.com/2016/02/white-people-emotions-tears/.

57   *If you cry and feel* Robin DiAngelo, *White Fragility: Why It's So
Hard for White People to Talk About Racism* (Boston: Beacon Press,
2018), 136.

58   *A study of white allies* Adam W. Fingerhut and Emma R. Hardy, "Applying a Model of Volunteerism to Better Understand the Experiences of White Ally Activists," *Group Processes & Intergroup Relations* 23 no. 4 (April 2020): 344–60, https://doi.org/10.1177 /1368430219837345.

### Principle 3: Cultivate Curiosity

61   *Soon after the Oxford* Maureen Shaw, "The 8 Worst Mansplainers of 2014," *Mic*, December 3, 2014, https://www.mic.com/articles /105172/an-unscientific-ranking-of-the-year-s-worst-mansplainers.

64   *As Davidai and Gilovich* Shai Davidai and Thomas Gilovich, "The Headwinds/Tailwinds Asymmetry: An Availability Bias in Assessments of Barriers and Blessings," *Journal of Personality and Social Psychology* 111, no. 6 (December 2016): 835–51, https://doi.org /10.1037/pspa0000066.

65   *In a study of college students* Barbara Gray et al., "Identity Work by First-Generation College Students to Counteract Class-Based Microaggressions," *Organization Studies* 39, vol. 9 (September 2018): 1227–50, https://doi.org/10.1177/0170840617736935.

66   *No problem* "Sikhism: An Educator's Guide," the Sikh Coalition, accessed January 14, 2022, https://www.sikhcoalition.org/wp-content /uploads/2018/08/Sikhism-educator-guide.pdf.

66   *Again, the Intersex Campaign* "Intersex Campaign for Equality," Intersex Campaign for Equality, accessed January 14, 2022, https:// www.intersexequality.com/.

66   *In debates on topics* Brian Tashman, "Barton: Schools 'Force' Students 'To Be Homosexual,'" *Right Wing Watch*, August 5, 2011, https://www.rightwingwatch.org/post/barton-schools-force-students -to-be-homosexual/; "American College of Pediatricians Say 'Gender Ideology' Is Child Abuse," CBN News, March 20, 2016, https:// www1.cbn.com/cbnnews/us/2016/March/American-College-of -Pediatricians-Say-Gender-Ideology-Is-Child-Abuse.

66   *Sure enough, a quick search* "American College of Pediatricians," Southern Poverty Law Center, accessed January 14, 2022, https:// www.splcenter.org/fighting-hate/extremist-files/group/american -college-pediatricians.

67   *Ijeoma Oluo offers* Ijeoma Oluo, "Welcome to the Anti-Racism Movement—Here's What You've Missed," *Medium*, March 16, 2017,

https://medium.com/the-establishment/welcome-to-the-anti-racism
-movement-heres-what-you-ve-missed-711089cb7d34.

67   *Uma Narayan, an Indian philosopher* Uma Narayan, *Dislocating
Cultures: Identities, Traditions, and Third World Feminism* (New
York: Routledge, 1997), 132–33.

68   *Young quipped* Damon Young, "Yeah, Let's Not Talk About Race,"
*New York Times*, July 10, 2020, https://www.nytimes.com/2020
/07/10/opinion/george-floyd-racism.html.

68   *The late-night comedy program* "Educate Your White Friends with
Blacklexa," *The Daily Show*, June 27, 2020, YouTube video, 1:45,
https://www.youtube.com/watch?v=v6S3tjXxh40.

69   *People with disabilities* Perry Zurn, *Curiosity and Power: The Politics of Inquiry* (Minneapolis: University of Minnesota Press, 2021),
164, 182; Nik Moreno, "25 Ridiculous Questions and Comments
I've Heard About My Disability," *Wear Your Voice*, May 17, 2016,
https://www.wearyourvoicemag.com/25-ridiculous-questions
-comments-ive-heard-disability/.

70   *She added* Emily Kirkpatrick, "Zendaya Says Giuliana Rancic's Infamous Comment About Her Oscars Dreadlocks Made Her Think
About How She Could 'Have a Lasting Impact,'" *Vanity Fair*,
March 19, 2021, https://www.vanityfair.com/style/2021/03/zendaya
-giuliana-rancic-dreadlocks-comment-oscars-2015-w-magazine.

70   *Initially, Rancic dismissed* "Zendaya Revisits Giuliana Rancic
Dreadlocks Incident 6 Years Later," *TooFab*, March 17, 2021, https://
toofab.com/2021/03/17/zendaya-revists-giuliana-rancic-infamous
-remarks-about-her-dreadlocks/.

70   *In an on-air apology* Jack Linshi, "Giuliana Rancic Issues On-Air
Apology for Comments on Zendaya's Hair," *Time*, February 24,
2015, https://time.com/3721516/giuliana-rancic-zendaya-hair/.

71   *Some U.S. states* Janelle Griffith, "New York Is Second State to Ban
Discrimination Based on Natural Hairstyles," NBC News, July 15,
2019, https://www.nbcnews.com/news/nbcblk/new-york
-second-state-ban-discrimination-based-natural-hairstyles-n1029931.

71   *Sheldon responds The Big Bang Theory*, season 3, episode 2, "The
Jiminy Conjecture," directed by Mark Cendrowski, aired September 28, 2009, on CBS.

71   *As former United States secretary* Dan Zak, "'Nothing Ever Ends':
Sorting Through Rumsfeld's Knowns and Unknowns," *Washington
Post*, July 1, 2021, https://www.washingtonpost.com/lifestyle/style

/rumsfeld-dead-words-known-unknowns/2021/07/01/831175c2-d9df
-11eb-bb9e-70fda8c37057_story.html.

72 *They then tend to treat* Daniel Kahneman, *Thinking, Fast and Slow*
(New York: Farrar, Straus and Giroux, 2011), 201.

72 *Robert Livingston, the psychologist* Robert Livingston, *The Conver-
sation: How Seeking and Speaking the Truth About Racism Can
Radically Transform Individuals and Organizations* (New York:
Currency Press, 2021), 5–6.

72 *Researchers have discovered* Carmen Sanchez and David Dunning,
"Overconfidence Among Beginners: Is a Little Learning a Danger-
ous Thing?," *Journal of Personality and Social Psychology* 114, no. 1
(January 2018): 10–28, https://doi.org/10.1037/pspa0000102.

72 *With just "a little learning"* Ibid., 25.

73 *Dotson notes that she'd* Kristie Dotson, "Tracking Epistemic Violence, Tracking Practices of Silencing," *Hypatia* 26, no. 2 (Spring
2011): 236–57, http://www.jstor.org/stable/23016544.

74 *One study divided participants* Michael W. Kraus and Dacher
Keltner, "Signs of Socioeconomic Status: A Thin-Slicing Approach,"
*Psychological Science* 20, no. 1 (January 2009): 99–106, https://doi
.org/10.1111/j.1467-9280.2008.02251.x.

75 *In a classic cartoon* Riana Duncan cartoon, reproduced in Mary
Beard, *Women and Power* (New York: Liveright Publishing, 2017), 7.

76 *Some employees even joked* Susan Chira, "The Universal Phenomenon of Men Interrupting Women," *New York Times*, June 14, 2017,
https://www.nytimes.com/2017/06/14/business/women-sexism
-work-huffington-kamala-harris.html.

76 *Philosopher Miranda Fricker* Miranda Fricker, *Epistemic Injustice:
Power and the Ethics of Knowing* (New York: Oxford University
Press, 2007), 1.

76 *Fricker points out* Ibid., 48.

76 *And regardless, as Alcoff* Linda Martín Alcoff, "On Judging Epistemic Credibility: Is Social Identity Relevant?," in *Women of Color
and Philosophy*, ed. Naomi Zack (Oxford: Blackwell Publishers,
2000), 247–48.

76 *Women and people of color* Esther H. Chen et al., "Gender Disparity
in Analgesic Treatment of Emergency Department Patients with
Acute Abdominal Pain," *Academic Emergency Medicine* 15, no. 5
(May 2008): 414–18, doi: 10.1111/j.1553-2712.2008.00100.x; Kelly
M. Hoffman et al., "Racial Bias in Pain Assessment and Treatment

Recommendations, and False Beliefs About Biological Differences Between Blacks and Whites," *Proceedings of the National Academy of Sciences* 113, no. 16 (April 2016): 4296–301, doi: 10.1073/pnas .1516047113; Paulyne Lee et al., "Racial and Ethnic Disparities in the Management of Acute Pain in US Emergency Departments: Meta-Analysis and Systematic Review," *American Journal of Emergency Medicine* 37, no. 9 (September 2019): 1770–77, doi: 10.1016 /j.ajem.2019.06.014.

76   *Women entrepreneurs are less likely* Alison Wood Brooks et al., "Investors Prefer Entrepreneurial Ventures Pitched by Attractive Men," *Proceedings of the National Academy of Sceinces* 111, no. 12 (March 2014): 4427–31, https://doi.org/10.1073/pnas.1321202111.

77   *Bisexuals are often viewed* Michael Castleman, "The Continuing Controversy Over Bisexuality," *Psychology Today*, March 15, 2016, https://www.psychologytoday.com/us/blog/all-about-sex/201603 /the-continuing-controversy-over-bisexuality; Benoit Denizet-Lewis, "The Scientific Quest to Prove Bisexuality Exists," *New York Times Magazine*, March 20, 2014, https://www.nytimes.com /2014/03/23/magazine/the-scientific-quest-to-prove-bisexuality -exists.html.

77   *Trans people are sometimes* German Lopez, "Myth #1: Transgender People Are Confused or Tricking Others," *Vox*, November 14, 2018, https://www.vox.com/identities/2016/5/13/17938090/transgender -people-tricks-confused; Shayla Love, "The WHO Says Being Transgender Is a Mental Illness. But That's About to Change," *Washington Post*, July 28, 2016, https://www.washingtonpost.com/news /morning-mix/wp/2016/07/28/the-w-h-o-says-being-transgender -is-a-mental-illness-but-thats-about-to-change/.

77   *It's not only that* Fricker, *Epistemic Injustice*, 17.

77   *As writer Upton Sinclair* Upton Sinclair, *I, Candidate for Governor: And How I Got Licked* (Berkeley: University of California Press, 1994), 109.

77   *In an interview with researchers* Jerome Rabow et al., *Ending Racism in America: One Microaggression at a Time* (Dubuque, IA: Kendall Hunt Publishing Company, 2014), 189. See also Derald Wing Sue, *Race Talk and the Conspiracy of Silence: Understanding and Facilitating Difficult Dialogues on Race* (Hoboken: John Wiley & Sons, 2015), 131–32.

78   *Reni Eddo-Lodge describes* Reni Eddo-Lodge, "Why I'm No Longer

Talking to White People About Race," accessed January 14, 2022, https://renieddolodge.co.uk/why-im-no-longer-talking-to-white -people-about-race/. Paradoxically, the success of Eddo-Lodge's blog post caused her to have many more conversations about race, cul- minating in a bestselling book of the same title: Reni Eddo-Lodge, *Why I'm No Longer Talking to White People About Race* (New York: Bloomsbury Publishing, 2017).

79    *She says to consider* Fricker, *Epistemic Injustice*, 91.

79    *In that situation, philosopher* Louise Antony, "Sisters, Please, I'd Rather Do It Myself: A Defense of Individualism in Feminist Epis- temology," *Philosophical Topics* 23, no. 2 (Fall 1995): 59, 89, https:// www.jstor.org/stable/43154208.

### Principle 4: Disagree Respectfully

86    *In a prominent work* Sherif Girgis, Ryan T. Anderson, and Robert P. George, *What Is Marriage? Man and Woman: A Defense* (New York: Encounter Books, 2012), 10.

86    *"The question is"* CNN, "Orman and Anderson on Same-Sex Mar- riage," March 27, 2013, video, 3:21, https://www.cnn.com /videos/bestoftv/2013/03/27/pmt-ryan-anderson-suze-orman -same-sex-marriage.cnn.

88    *And you'll find it excruciating* Richard J. Herrnstein and Charles Murray, *The Bell Curve: Intelligence and Class Structure in American Life* (New York: Free Press, 1994), chaps. 13–15.

90    *But as philosopher Daniel Dennett* Daniel C. Dennett, *Intuition Pumps and Other Tools for Thinking* (London: Penguin Books, 2013), 34.

90    *The letter's signatories slammed* "A Letter on Justice and Open De- bate," *Harper's Magazine*, July 7, 2020, https://harpers.org/a-letter -on-justice-and-open-debate/.

91    *In the influential book* Douglas Stone, Bruce Patton, and Sheila Heen, *Difficult Conversations: How to Discuss What Matters Most*, 10th anniversary ed. (New York: Penguin Books, 2010), 94–103.

92    *Behavioral scientist Xuan Zhao* Xuan Zhao et al., "How to Disagree Productively and Find Common Ground? The Power of Express- ing Gratitude," Chicago Booth Center for Decision Research— Experiment Debriefing, May 4, 2019, https://www.xuan-zhao.com /uploads/5/6/1/6/5616522/tyb_debriefing_sheet.pdf; Xuan Zhao,

Heather Caruso, and Jane Risen, "'Thank You, Because . . .': Discussing Differences While Finding Common Ground" (conference paper, 2020), https://www.xuan-zhao.com/uploads/5/6/1/6/5616522 /thank_you_because_aom2020_submission.pdf.

92 *Other research shows* Silke Eschert and Bernd Simon, "Respect and Political Disagreement: Can Intergroup Respect Reduce the Biased Evaluation of Outgroup Arguments?," *PLOS ONE* 14, no. 3 (March 2019), https://doi.org/10.1371/journal.pone.0211556.

92 *Dave Isay, a radio producer* Norah O'Donnell, "Bridging America's Political Divide with Conversations, 'One Small Step' at a Time," CBS News, January 9, 2022, https://www.cbsnews.com/news/one -small-step-storycorps-60-minutes-2022-01-10/.

93 *One such parent is* Andy Pierrotti, "These Parents Questioned Critical Race Theory and DEI Programs in Public Schools. They Interviewed Experts and Here's What They Found," 11Alive, October 4, 2021, https://www.11alive.com/article/news/investigations /drawing-conclusions/cherokee-county-ga-parents-skeptical-critical -race-theory-dei-speak-to-experts/85-8a198b32-ad58-45bc-956f -563b8b5dce90.

93 *Yet in their hour-long conversation* Carol Anderson, Bart Glasgow, and Coley Glasgow, "Parents Skeptical of Critical Race Theory Talk to Experts: Drawing Conclusions PART 1 FULL INTV," 11Alive, October 4, 2021, YouTube video, 1:00:01, https://www.youtube.com /watch?v=mmRO3J6IJC8.

96 *Writer Moira Weigel* Moira Weigel, "Reasonable Men Calming You Down with Moira Weigel," October 13, 2018, in *The Dig*, podcast, 46:06 at 16:30, https://www.thedigradio.com/podcast/reasonable -men-calming-you-down-with-moira-weigel/.

96 *A comic by Randall Munroe* Randall Munroe, "Duty Calls," *xkcd*, accessed April 25, 2022, https://xkcd.com/386/.

98 *Quotas are a well-established practice* Melanie M. Hughes et al., "Gender Quotas for Legislatures and Corporate Boards," *Annual Review of Sociology* 43 (July 2017): 331–52, https://doi.org/10.1146 /annurev-soc-060116-053324.

98 *The second example* Michael Edison Hayden, "Women Shouldn't Have the Right to Vote, Says 'Alt-Right' Leader Richard Spencer," *Newsweek*, October 14, 2017, https://www.newsweek.com/alt-right -leader-richard-spencer-isnt-sure-if-women-should-be-allowed-vote -685048.

98 *According to Damore* James Damore, "Google's Ideological Echo Chamber" (unpublished manuscript, July 2017), https://assets .documentcloud.org/documents/3914586/Googles-Ideological-Echo -Chamber.pdf.

102 *In her view, speaking* Suzanne Nossel, *Dare to Speak: Defending Free Speech for All* (New York: Dey Street: 2020), 14.

**Principle 5: Apologize Authentically**

105 *The man's apology describes* V (formerly known as Eve Ensler), *The Apology* (New York: Bloomsbury Publishing, 2019), 58–59.

105 *"You moved like a ghost"* Ibid., 50.

105 *The man takes full responsibility* Ibid., 64

105 *"You did not and could not"* Ibid., 108.

106 *He concludes* Ibid., 112.

106 *In a TED talk* V (formerly known as Eve Ensler), "The Profound Power of an Authentic Apology," TED, January 7, 2020, YouTube video, 8:23, https://www.youtube.com/watch?v=gQ-0oR3C1UM. While this apology met V's own standards for a successful apology, we recognize that not all survivors would necessarily appreciate this form of apology and might prefer other kinds of amends.

106 *Psychiatrist Aaron Lazare* Aaron Lazare, *On Apology* (New York: Oxford University Press, 2004), 255–56.

106 *Channeling her father's voice* V, *The Apology*, 9.

106 *"When a child hurts"* Molly Howes, *A Good Apology: Four Steps to Make Things Right* (New York: Grand Central Publishing, 2020), 42.

107 *As psychologist Harriet Lerner* Harriet Lerner, *Why Won't You Apologize? Healing Big Betrayals and Everyday Hurts* (New York: Simon & Schuster, 2017), 175.

107 *Consultant John Kador* John Kador, *Effective Apology: Mending Fences, Building Bridges, and Restoring Trust* (San Francisco: Berrett-Koehler, 2009), 3.

107 *"In some cases"* Ibid., 30.

108 *Yet in a series of bombshell* Krystie Lee Yandoli, "Former Employees Say Ellen's 'Be Kind' Talk Show Mantra Masks a Toxic Work Culture," *BuzzFeed*, July 16, 2020, https://www.buzzfeednews.com /article/krystieyandoli/ellen-employees-allege-toxic-workplace -culture; Krystie Lee Yandoli, "Dozens of Former 'Ellen Show' Employees Say Executive Producers Engaged in Rampant Sexual Misconduct and Harassment," *BuzzFeed*, July 30, 2020, https://

www.buzzfeednews.com/article/krystieyandoli/ex-ellen-show
-employees-sexual-misconduct-allegations.

108  *She then said curtly* John Koblin, "Ellen DeGeneres Returns to
Show with Apology for Toxic Workplace," *New York Times*, May 12,
2021, https://www.nytimes.com/2020/09/21/business/media/ellen
-degeneres-show.html.

108  *Later in the monologue* Winston Gieseke, "In California: A Huge
Backlog of Unemployment Claims, and Ellen Says She's Sorry," *USA
Today*, September 21, 2020, https://www.usatoday.com/story
/news/nation/2020/09/21/snow-fire-ellen-degeneres-emmy-awards
-schitts-creek-ruth-bader-ginsburg/5855951002/.

108  *One outlet panned* Kevin Fallon, "Ellen's Strange 'Apology' Won't
Satisfy Anybody," *Daily Beast*, September 21, 2020, https://www
.thedailybeast.com/ellen-degeneres-strange-apology-for-toxic
-behavior-wont-satisfy-anybody; Annabelle Spranklen, "Ellen
DeGeneres Might Have Just Given the Worst Apology of All Time
Making Us Question, Is She Really That Sorry?," *Glamour*, September 22, 2020, https://www.glamourmagazine.co.uk/article/ellen
-degeneres-show-apology.

108  *DeGeneres's apology is an example* Annie Finch, "How to Apologize
in a Way That Actually Works," *Medium*, March 12, 2019, https://
medium.com/@AnnieFinch/how-to-apologize-in-a-way-that-actually
-works-b863f6487a70.

108  *"The liberation is in the details"* V, "The Profound Power of an
Authentic Apology," TED, January 7, 2020, YouTube video, 8:23,
https://www.youtube.com/watch?v=gQ-0oR3C1UM.

109  *In a TV interview* "Woman Hedges Apology in Tense Interview on
Hotel Attack," AP News, January 12, 2021, https://apnews.com/article
/miya-ponsetto-hedges-apology-ec4aed792689d22aeedc4e369b298474.

109  *Ponsetto said the following year* Tamar Lapin, "'Soho Karen' Miya
Ponsetto Wishes She 'Apologized Differently' to Keyon Harrold Jr.,"
*New York Post*, November 8, 2021, https://nypost.com/2021/11/08
/soho-karen-miya-ponsetto-wishes-she-apologized-differently/.

110  *Like Lerner, we admire* Lerner, *Why Won't You Apologize?*, 106–7.

110  *Anne Hathaway, who played* Marianne Garvey, "Anne Hathaway
Apologizes to Disability Community amid 'The Witches' Backlash,"
*CNN Entertainment*, November 6, 2020, https://www.cnn.com
/2020/11/06/entertainment/anne-hathaway-apologizes-witches-trnd
/index.html.

111   *The reaction was immediate* Lesley Messer, "Sara Gilbert Rips Roseanne Barr's 'Abhorrent' Tweets," *ABC News*, May 29, 2018, https://abcnews.go.com/US/sara-gilbert-rips-roseanne-barrs -abhorrent-tweets/story?id=55509934.

111   *This bizarre observation* Sam Wolfson, "Sorry, Not Sorry: A Time-line of Roseanne Barr's Responses to Her Firing," *Guardian*, July 27, 2018, https://www.theguardian.com/culture/2018/jul/27 /roseanne-barr-apology-timeline.

111   *She also included the disclaimer* Leslie Turk, "Racist Remarks Captured in Video of Lafayette Judge's Family Cheering Footage of Foiled Burglary," *Current*, December 13, 2021, https://thecurrentla .com/2021/racist-remarks-captured-in-video-of-lafayette-judges -family-cheering-footage-of-foiled-burglary/.

112   *Sports announcer Matt Rowan* Maria Cramer, "Announcer Caught on Open Mic Using Racial Slur at Basketball Game," *New York Times*, March 13, 2021, https://www.nytimes.com/2021/03/13/us /norman-oklahoma-announcer-matt-rowan.html.

112   *When a critic called her out* Franchesca Ramsey, "Getting Called Out: How to Apologize," chescaleigh, September 6, 2013, YouTube video, 8:36, https://www.youtube.com/watch?v=C8xJXKYL8pU.

113   *In a representative essay* Jamie Utt, "Intent vs. Impact: Why Your Intentions Don't Really Matter," *Everyday Feminism*, July 30, 2013, https://everydayfeminism.com/2013/07/intentions-dont-really -matter/.

113   *As jurist Oliver Wendell Holmes* Oliver Wendell Holmes Jr., *The Common Law*, American Bar Association Edition (Chicago: ABA, 2009), 2.

113   *High-school teacher Andrew Puckey* Elizabeth Doran, "Oneida County Teacher Apologizes for Saying 'All Lives Matter' at High School Ceremony," Syracuse.com, June 16, 2020, https://www .syracuse.com/schools/2020/06/oneida-county-teacher-apologizes -for-saying-all-lives-matter-at-high-school-ceremony.html.

114   *Actor Arthur Chu* German Lopez, "Why You Should Stop Saying 'All Lives Matter,' Explained in 9 Different Ways," *Vox*, July 11, 2016, https://www.vox.com/2016/7/11/12136140/black-all-lives-matter.

114   *Then she apologized* Todd Martens, "Madonna Issues Apology for Using N-Word on Instagram," *Chicago Tribune*, January 18, 2014, https://www.chicagotribune.com/entertainment/chi-madonna -nword-instagram-20140118-story.html.

114  *English women's football coach* "I Am Not a Sexist, Says England Women's Coach Neville," Reuters, January 29, 2018, https://www.reuters.com/article/uk-soccer-england-women-neville/i-am-not-a-sexist-says-england-womens-coach-neville-idUKKBN1FI1Q2 (edited to conform to American spelling).

114  *David Simms, a hockey commentator* Alex Bollinger, "Hockey Commentator Makes Non-Apology for Homophobic Kiss Cam 'Joke,'" *LGBTQ Nation*, March 9, 2017, https://www.lgbtqnation.com/2017/03/hockey-executive-makes-non-apology-homophobic-joke/.

115  *Initially, like the others* "Hannah Brown Used the N-Word on Instagram Live and *Bachelorette* Fans Are Furious," *Glamour*, May 17, 2020, https://www.glamour.com/story/hannah-brown-n-word-instagram-live-twitter-reactions.

116  *Brown then addressed her fans* Hannah Brown, "Hannah Brown Full Instagram Live Apology," Sarah B, May 30, 2020, YouTube video, 14:15, https://www.youtube.com/watch?v=Rq-Z4lPO9r4.

116  *"I'm a comedian who pushes boundaries"* Laura Bradley, "*SNL* Hire Shane Gillis Doesn't Quite Apologize for Racist, Homophobic Remarks," *Vanity Fair*, September 13, 2019, https://www.vanityfair.com/hollywood/2019/09/snl-shane-gillis-racist-homophobic-remarks-response.

117  *At the end of the post* Jamie DuCharme, "Mario Batali's Sexual Misconduct Apology Came with a Cinnamon Roll Recipe," *Time*, December 16, 2017, https://time.com/5067633/mario-batali-cinnamon-rolls-apology/.

117  *As Zheng points out* Rebecca Knight, "You've Been Called Out for a Microaggression. What Do You Do?," *Harvard Business Review*, July 24, 2020, https://hbr.org/2020/07/youve-been-called-out-for-a-microaggression-what-do-you-do.

118  *"We make fun of everyone"* Dave Itzkoff, "Why Hank Azaria Won't Play Apu on 'The Simpsons' Anymore," *New York Times*, February 25, 2020, https://www.nytimes.com/2020/02/25/arts/television/hank-azaria-simpsons-apu.html.

118  *He knew from his recovery* Hank Azaria, "Hank Azaria," April 12, 2021, in *Armchair Expert with Dax Shepard*, podcast, 1:41:41 at 45:04 to 56:05, https://armchairexpertpod.com/pods/hank-azaria.

119  *The mayor stated* Vi Lyles, "Charlotte Mayor Vi Lyles Apologizes for Past Discrimination," Qcitymetro, August 12, 2020, YouTube video, 5:33, https://www.youtube.com/watch?v=1GrkjpkSJao.

119  *Yet as the* Charlotte Observer Danielle Chemtob, "Racial Equity Talks in Charlotte: Not Deep. Not Justice. Not Enough, Advocates Say," *Charlotte Observer,* February 17, 2021, https://www.charlotte observer.com/news/local/article248797480.html.

119  *As author Stephen Covey* Tom Fox, "Stephen M. R. Covey's Guide to Building Trust," *Washington Post,* July 18, 2013, https://www.washingtonpost.com/news/on-leadership/wp/2013/07/18/stephen-m-r-coveys-guide-to-building-trust/.

119  *Unsurprisingly, research indicates* Robert D. Carlisle et al., "Do Actions Speak Louder Than Words? Differential Effects of Apology and Restitution on Behavioral and Self-Report Measures of Forgiveness," *Journal of Positive Psychology* 7, no. 4 (May 2012): 294–305, https://doi.org/10.1080/17439760.2012.690444.

120  *Molly Howes observes that* Howes, *A Good Apology,* 100–101.

120  *"We are the true Hebrews"* Seth Cohen, "Nick Cannon's YouTube Show Causes Waves," *Forbes,* July 13, 2020, https://www.forbes.com/sites/sethcohen/2020/07/13/nick-cannon-spreads-anti-jewish-theories-criticizing-rothschilds-and-zionists/.

121  *Noting that he'd received* Abel Shifferaw, "Nick Cannon Issues Apology to Jewish Community for His 'Hurtful and Divisive Words,'" *Complex,* July 15, 2020, https://www.complex.com/pop-culture/2020/07/nick-cannon-apologizes-to-jewish-community-for-hurtful-anti-semitic-comments.

121  *One such learning experience* Trace William Cowen, "Nick Cannon and Rabbi Abraham Cooper Sit Down for Extended Interview on Dangers of Anti-Semitism," *Complex,* July 21, 2020, https://www.complex.com/pop-culture/2020/07/nick-cannon-rabbi-abraham-cooper-sit-down-for-extended-interview-on-anti-semitism.

121  *During that conversation, Cannon* Nick Cannon, "[FULL SESSION] Rabbi Abraham Cooper on Cannon's Class," Nick Cannon, July 21, 2020, YouTube video, 1:19:30 at 4:14, https://www.youtube.com/watch?v=xdJ2yO7HFMM&t=1634s.

121  *Reflecting on his experience* Rabbi Noam E. Marans, "I Spoke to Nick Cannon About Anti-Semitism. This Is What I Learned," *Jewish Telegraphic Agency,* August 17, 2020, https://www.jta.org/2020/08/17/opinion/i-spoke-to-nick-cannon-about-anti-semitism-this-is-what-i-learned.

121  *As Cannon himself put it* Nick Cannon, "Nick Cannon on Making Amends After Anti-Semitic Comments," ABC News, March 16,

2021, YouTube video, 7:34 at 2:07, https://www.youtube.com
/watch?v=6_bITYsrWSg.

122 *After taking a hiatus* Jordan Moreau, "'The Good Place' Producer Megan Amram Vows to 'Invoke Change' in Social Media Return," *Variety*, October 27, 2020, https://variety.com/2020/tv/news/megan -amram-good-place-twitter-1234816773/.

122 *This representation frustrated some* "'Unbreakable Kimmy Schmidt' Has Two Native American Actors. It Needed Three," *Indian Country Today*, March 12, 2015, https://indiancountrytoday .com/archive/unbreakable-kimmy-schmidt-has-two-native -american-actors-it-needed-three.

122 *Comedian Tina Fey* Jackson McHenry, "Tina Fey Is 'Opting Out' of Apologizing for Controversies: 'My New Goal Is Not to Explain Jokes,'" *Vulture*, December 20, 2015, https://www.vulture.com/2015 /12/tina-fey-is-opting-out-of-explaining-her-jokes.html.

122 *A few years later* Cole Delbyck, "Tina Fey Agrees She 'Screwed Up' 'SNL' Sketch About Charlottesville," *HuffPost*, May 5, 2018, https:// www.huffpost.com/entry/tina-fey-says-she-screwed-up-snl-sketch -about-charlottesville_n_5aec7cd6e4b0c4f193221323.

123 *"I understand now that"* Will Thorne, "'30 Rock' Blackface Episodes Pulled from Streaming, Syndication at Tina Fey and NBCU's Request," *Variety*, June 22, 2020, https://variety.com/2020/tv/news /30-rock-blackface-episodes-removed-tina-fey-1234645607/.

## Principle 6: Apply the Platinum Rule

127 *What then unfolded* Matt Novak, "Racist Tech CEO Harasses Family at Dinner: 'Trump's Gonna Fuck You,'" *Gizmodo*, July 8, 2020, https://gizmodo.com/racist-tech-ceo-harasses-family-at-dinner -trumps-gonna-1844303275; "Solid8 CEO Michael Lofthouse Goes Off on Racist Rant at Asian American Family in Carmel Valley|ABC7," ABC7, July 7, 2020, YouTube video, 0:51, https:// www.youtube.com/watch?v=FaSMvJ4opAE.

128 *"If you see something"* Melanie Woodrow, "EXCLUSIVE: Waitress Who Stopped SF Tech CEO's Racist Rant at Carmel Valley Restaurant Shares What Happened," ABC7 News, July 8, 2020, https:// abc7news.com/tech-ceo-racist-rant-solid8-michael-lofthouse-in -carmel-gennica-cochran/6307544/.

129 *When Massachusetts senator* Will Weissert, "Warren's Outreach

to Black Voters Could Help VP Standing," AP News, June 16, 2020, https://apnews.com/article/deae262c0c22217cadc446affa4f4705.

129 *Our own institution* "Solidarity Week," NYU, accessed November 4, 2021, https://www.nyu.edu/life/events-traditions/solidarity-week.html.

129 *Activist Kim Tran* Ada Tseng, "What Solidarity Is and How You Can Practice It," *Los Angeles Times*, August 11, 2021, https://www.latimes .com/lifestyle/story/2021-08-11/what-is-definition-solidarity-how -can-practice-it.

131 *Writer Caitlin Deen Fair* Michael S. Kimmel and Abby L. Ferber, *Privilege: A Reader* (Boulder: Westview Press, 2016), 291–92.

131 *As our NYU colleague* Kwame Anthony Appiah, "Stonewall and the Myth of Self-Deliverance," *New York Times*, June 22, 2019, https:// www.nytimes.com/2019/06/22/opinion/sunday/stonewall-myth.html.

131 *What we can offer* Dave Kerpen, *The Art of People: 11 Simple People Skills That Will Get You Everything You Want* (New York: Portfolio Penguin, 2016), 95–98.

132 *She looks up to see* Harper Lee, *To Kill a Mockingbird*, 1st Perennial Classics ed. (New York: Perennial, 2002), 241; *To Kill a Mockingbird*, directed by Robert Mulligan (Universal Pictures, 1962), https://www.amazon.com/Kill-Mockingbird-Gregory-Peck /dp/B000I9VOO4.

132 *Sociologist Matthew Hughey* Matthew Hughey, *The White Savior Film: Content, Critics, and Consumption* (Philadelphia: Temple University Press, 2014), 13.

132 *As Hughey explains* Ibid., 1.

133 *On the other side* Ibid., 41, 48.

133 *The white savior liberates* Ibid., 41.

133 *In a rollicking parody* "White Savior: The Movie Trailer," *Late Night with Seth Meyers*, February 21, 2019, YouTube video, 5:51, https:// www.youtube.com/watch?v=T_RTnuJvg6U.

134 *A disability advocate* Andrew Pulrang, "3 Ways Disability Allyship Can Go Off Track," *Forbes*, April 14, 2021, https://www.forbes.com /sites/andrewpulrang/2021/04/14/3-ways-disability-allyship-can -go-off-track/.

134 *Experts on male allyship* W. Brad Johnson and David G. Smith, "How Men Can Become Better Allies to Women," *Harvard Business Review*, October 12, 2018, https://hbr.org/2018/10/how-men -can-become-better-allies-to-women.

134 *Among other critiques* Casira Copes, "How to Make Sure Your Ac-

tivism Is More Than Just Virtue Signaling," *An Injustice!*, February 17, 2021, https://aninjusticemag.com/how-to-make-sure-your -activism-is-more-than-just-virtue-signaling-7bc9df3f1ae0; The Angry Black Woman, "Things You Need To Understand #9— You Don't Get a Cookie," *The Angry Black Woman* (blog), April 29, 2008, http://theangryblackwoman.com/2008/04/29/no-cookie/.

134 *As racial justice advocate* Nova Reid, *The Good Ally: A Guided Anti-Racism Journey from Bystander to Changemaker* (London: HQ, 2021), 50.

134 *Participants who thought the ally* Charles Chu, "Target Percep-tions of Prejudice Confrontations: The Effect of Confronter Group Membership on Perceptions of Confrontation Motive and Target Empowerment" (master's thesis, Purdue University, 2017), https:// scholarworks.iupui.edu/handle/1805/12347. See also Mason D. Burns and Erica L. Granz, "'Sincere White People, Work in Con-junction with Us': Racial Minorities' Perceptions of White Ally Sincerity and Perceptions of Ally Efforts," *Group Processes and Intergroup Relations* (January 2022), https://doi.org/10.1177 /13684302211059699.

134 *A separate study* Joan M. Ostrove and Kendrick T. Brown, "Are Allies Who We Think They Are? A Comparative Analysis," *Journal of Applied Social Psychology* 48, no. 4 (April 2018): 195–204, https:// doi.org/10.1111/jasp.12502.

135 *But he distrusted his own instinct* Charles McNulty, "Aaron Sorkin Talks 'To Kill a Mockingbird' and Disavowing the White Savior Role," *Los Angeles Times*, April 30, 2019, https://www.latimes.com /entertainment/arts/la-et-cm-aaron-sorkin-kill-mockingbird -20190430-story.html.

136 *One foundational study* Monica E. Schneider et al., "Social Stigma and the Potential Costs of Assumptive Help," *Personality and So-cial Psychology Bulletin* 22, no. 2 (1996): 201–9.

136 *Another study in Israel* Samer Halabi, Arie Nadler, and John Dovi-dio, "Reactions to Receiving Assumptive Help: The Moderating Ef-fects of Group Membership and Perceived Need for Help," *Journal of Applied Social Psychology* 41, no. 12 (December 2011): 2793–815, https://doi.org/10.1111/j.1559-1816.2011.00859.x.

138 *Despite experiencing a concussion* Anthony Abraham Jack, *The Privileged Poor: How Elite Colleges Are Failing Disadvantaged Stu-dents* (Massachusetts: Harvard University Press, 2019), 93–95.

138   *United States Supreme Court* Sonia Sotomayor, "Sonia
        Sotomayor—'Just Ask' & Life as a Supreme Court Justice," *The
        Daily Show,* September 23, 2019, YouTube video, 22:51, https://www
        .youtube.com/watch?v=Nztz3yuF3lY.

139   *As psychologist Katie Wang* Katie Wang et al., "Independent or Un-
        grateful? Consequences of Confronting Patronizing Help for People
        with Disabilities," *Group Processes and Intergroup Relations* 18, no.
        4 (July 2015): 489–503, https://doi.org/10.1177/1368430214550345.

139   *In a study of elderspeak* Kristine N. Williams et al., "Elderspeak
        Communication: Impact on Dementia Care," *American Journal
        of Alzheimer's Disease and Other Dementias* 24, no. 1 (February–
        March 2009): 11–20.

140   *Some contrasted the image* Daniel Victor, "Pepsi Pulls Ad Accused
        of Trivializing Black Lives Matter," *New York Times,* April 5, 2017,
        https://www.nytimes.com/2017/04/05/business/kendall-jenner
        -pepsi-ad.html.

140   Riverdale *actor Lili Reinhart* Jenna Amatulli, "Lili Reinhart Apol-
        ogizes for Her Sideboob Photo Demanding Justice for Breonna
        Taylor," *HuffPost,* June 30, 2020, https://www.huffpost.com/entry
        /lili-reinhart-breonna-taylor-justice_n_5efb9341c5b612083c53ec2c.

141   *One world-weary observer* Charles Bramesco (@intothecrevasse),
        "We have entered a thrilling transitional phase in which the celebs
        have resumed thirst posting but have not yet stopped social justice
        posting, resulting in wondrous juxtapositions like this one from
        TV's Hot Betty yesterday," Twitter, June 29, 2020, https://twitter
        .com/intothecrevasse/status/1277699281890222080?lang=en.

141   *As one commenter noted* Graham Gremore, "Straight White Influ-
        encer Posts Sexy Gay Pride Selfie to Support Black Lives
        Matter . . . Wait, What?," *Queerty,* June 4, 2020, https://www
        .queerty.com/straight-white-influencer-posts-sexy-gay-pride-selfie
        -support-black-lives-matter-wait-20200604.

141   *The allyship photo shoot* Jenny Singer, "White Women: Stop Treat-
        ing Protests as Instagram Photo Shoots," *Glamour,* June 9, 2020,
        https://www.glamour.com/story/white-women-stop-treating
        -protests-as-instagram-photoshoots.

141   *"Posting a black square"* Natasha Noman, "'Blackout Tuesday' on
        Instagram Was a Teachable Moment for Allies Like Me," *NBC
        News,* June 6, 2020, https://www.nbcnews.com/think/opinion
        /blackout-tuesday-instagram-was-teachable-moment-allies-me

-ncna1225961; Nicole Rovine, "Engage in Non-Optical Allyship for Black Lives Matter," *Cornell Daily Sun*, June 7, 2020, https://cornellsun .com/2020/06/07/engage-in-non-optical-allyship-for-black-lives -matter/.

141  *As Ben Platt's character The Premise*, season 1, episode 1, "Social Justice Sex Tape," directed by B. J. Novak, aired September 16, 2021, on FX.

141  *Even the Spanish postal service* "Spain's New Postage Stamps Were Meant to Call Out Racism. Instead They Drew Outrage," NPR, May 28, 2021, https://www.npr.org/2021/05/28/1001228126/spains-new -postage-stamps-were-meant-to-call-out-racism-instead-they-drew -outrage.

142  *He pointed out the contradiction* Raphael Minder, "Spain Issued 'Equality Stamps' in Skin Tones. The Darker Ones Were Worth Less," *New York Times*, May 28, 2021, https://www.nytimes.com/2021 /05/28/world/europe/spain-stamps-racism.html.

144  *Social psychologists* Mahzarin Banaji and Anthony Greenwald, *Blindspot: Hidden Biases of Good People* (New York: Bantam Books, 2013), 152.

144  *Behavioral economist Iris Bohnet* Iris Bohnet, *What Works: Gender Equality by Design* (Cambridge: Harvard University Press, 2016), 1–2.

144  *After conducting a few* "11 Harmful Types of Unconscious Bias and How to Interrupt Them (Blog Post)," *Catalyst*, January 2, 2020, https://www.catalyst.org/2020/01/02/interrupt-unconscious-bias/.

145  *He decided to follow* Bohnet, *What Works*, 123–45.

146  *You could employ* Charles Duhigg, *Smarter, Faster, Better: The Transformative Power of Real Productivity* (New York: Random House, 2016), 70.

146  *If you're a facilitator* Bohnet, *What Works*, 179.

146  *Sociologist Anthony Abraham Jack* Jack, *The Privileged Poor*, 173.

146  *Jack offered an alternative* Ibid., 178.

**Principle 7: Be Generous to the Source**

155  *In a recent conversation* Devrupa Rakshit, "Why Disability Activists Argue Against Labels Like 'Differently Abled,'" *Swaddle*, June 17, 2021, https://theswaddle.com/why-people-with-disabilities-often -prefer-to-be-called-disabled-over-differently-abled/.

156  *News anchor Chris Hayes* Sean Illing, "Chris Hayes on Escaping the 'Doom Loop' of Trump's Presidency," *Vox*, April 19, 2017, https://

www.vox.com/2017/4/19/15356534/chris-hayes-donald-trump-media
-elections-2016-criminal-justice.

156   *Ultimately, we agree* bell hooks, interview by Maya Angelou, *Sham-bhala Sun*, January 1998, http://www.hartford-hwp.com/archives
/45a/249.html.

157   *The Supreme Court rejected Snyder v. Phelps*, 562 U.S. 443 (2011).

158   *Our colleague Bryan Stevenson* Francesca Trianni, "Bryan Stevenson: 'Believe Things You Haven't Seen,'" *Time*, June 19, 2015,
https://time.com/collection-post/3928285/bryan-stevenson-interview
-time-100/.

158   *As he explains* Bryan Stevenson, "Bryan Stevenson on the Legacy
of Enslavement," in *Vox Conversations*, podcast, October 7, 2021,
1:03:44 at 27:23, https://pod.link/voxconversations/episode
/77c27191729412ee63fda359cdcc2a69.

158   *Professor of social work* Brené Brown, *Dare to Lead* (New York:
Random House, 2018), 128–29.

158   *Just as they're the expert* Douglas Stone, Bruce Patton, and Sheila
Heen, *Difficult Conversations: How to Discuss What Matters Most*,
10th anniversary ed. (New York: Penguin Books, 2010), 53–54.

158   *These comments angered* Abby Phillip, "Tulsa's Black Residents
Grapple with the City's Racist History and Police Brutality Ahead
of Trump's Rally," *CNN*, June 16, 2020, https://www.cnn.com
/2020/06/16/politics/tulsa-oklahoma-history-race/index.html.

158   *A few days later* Andrea Eger, "Tulsa Mayor Apologizes for His
'Dumb and Overly-Simplistic' Comment on Terence Crutcher Killing," *Tulsa World*, June 11, 2020, https://tulsaworld.com/news
/local/government-and-politics/tulsa-mayor-apologizes-for-his
-dumb-and-overly-simplistic-comment-on-terence-crutcher-killing
/article_f369969c-bdce-5b64-9127-6c0efb3647db.html.

160   *Psychologist Scott Plous* S. Plous, "Responding to Overt Displays
of Prejudice: A Role-Playing Exercise," *Teaching of Psychology* 27,
no. 3 (August 2000): 198–200, https://doi.org/10.1207/S15328023
TOP2703_07.

161   *In offering this self-disclosure* Dolly Chugh, *The Person You Mean to
Be: How Good People Fight Bias* (New York: HarperCollins, 2018), 212.

161   *She observes that this strategy* Amy C. Edmondson, *The Fearless
Organization: Creating Psychological Safety in the Workplace for
Learning, Innovation, and Growth* (Hoboken: John Wiley & Sons,
2019), xvi.

161  *In an article titled* Benoît Monin, "Holier Than Me? Threatening Social Comparison in the Moral Domain," *Revue Internationale de Psychologie Sociale* 50, no. 1 (2007): 53–68.

162  *One of Monin's studies* Julia A. Minson and Benoît Monin, "Do-Gooder Derogation: Disparaging Morally Motivated Minorities to Defuse Anticipated Reproach," *Social Psychological and Personality Science* 3, no. 2 (March 2012): 200–207, https://doi.org/10.1177/1948550611415695.

162  *In another Monin study* Benoît Monin et al., "The Rejection of Moral Rebels: Resenting Those Who Do the Right Thing," *Journal of Personality and Social Psychology* 95, no. 1 (July 2008): 76–93, doi: 10.1037/0022-3514.95.1.76.

163  *In a study about homophobia* Larry R. Martinez et al., "Standing Up and Speaking Out Against Prejudice Toward Gay Men in the Workplace," *Journal of Vocational Behavior* 103(A), no. 71 (December 2017): 71–85, https://doi.org/10.1016/j.jvb.2017.08.001.

164  *They experience "escalator wit"* The more formal term for this phenomenon is the French expression *l'esprit de l'escalier.* See Camille Chevalier-Karfis, "Meaning of the French Expression *Avoir L'Esprit D'Escalier*," ThoughtCo, April 5, 2017, https://www.thoughtco.com/meaning-french-expression-avoir-lesprit-descalier-1368730.

164  *To help you engage* Shakirah Bourne and Dana Alison Levy, eds., *Allies: Real Talk About Showing Up, Screwing Up, and Trying Again* (New York: DK Publishing, 2021), 229; Karen Catlin, *Better Allies: Everyday Actions to Create Inclusive, Engaging Workplaces* (USA: Better Allies Press, 2019), 83–84; Chugh, *The Person You Mean to Be*, 205–24; Diane J. Goodman, *Promoting Diversity and Social Justice: Educating People from Privileged Groups*, 2nd ed. (New York: Routledge, 2011), 166–70; David G. Smith and W. Brad Johnson, *Good Guys: How Men Can Be Better Allies for Women in the Workplace* (Boston: Harvard Business Review Press, 2020), 109–36.

166  *The video starts with* Sarah Maslin Nir, "White Woman Is Fired After Calling Police on Black Man in Central Park," *New York Times*, May 26, 2020, https://www.nytimes.com/2020/05/26/nyregion/amy-cooper-dog-central-park.html.

167  *After Christian Cooper's sister* Heidi Stevens, "Column: George Floyd, Killed in Minneapolis, Is Why Amy Cooper's Central Park Call Was So Repugnant," *Chicago Tribune*, May 27, 2020, https://

www.chicagotribune.com/columns/heidi-stevens/ct-heidi-stevens
-amy-cooper-george-floyd-weaponized-whiteness-0527-20200527
-voun4un45zarte3zdayulr573m-story.html; Melody Cooper,
"Chris Cooper Is My Brother. Here's Why I Posted His Video," *New
York Times*, May 31, 2020, https://www.nytimes.com/2020/05/31
/opinion/chris-cooper-central-park.html.

167  *Chugh offers the "20/60/20 rule"* Chugh, *The Person You Mean to
Be*, 209–11.

168  *Chugh observes that, in general* Dolly Chugh, "Ally: Individual
Strategies to Advance Diversity and Inclusion," NYU School of Law,
March 19, 2020, YouTube video, 57:48 at 24:18, https://www.youtube
.com/watch?v=o_4AB_JyHCg.

168  *Even Megan Phelps-Roper* Megan Phelps-Roper, "Sarah Sits Down
with an Ex-Member of the Westboro Baptist Church," *I Love You,
America*, October 25, 2017, YouTube video, 7:18, https://www
.youtube.com/watch?v=EmgZgHpv8Zs.

169  *In a course she teaches* Jessica Bennett, "What If Instead of Calling
People Out, We Called Them In?," *New York Times*, November 19,
2020, https://www.nytimes.com/2020/11/19/style/loretta-ross
-smith-college-cancel-culture.html.

169  *Ross had her own experience* Loretta J. Ross, "Loretta J. Ross: Don't
Call People Out—Call Them In," TED talk, August 4, 2021, YouTube
video, 14:18, https://www.youtube.com/watch?v=xw_720iQDss.

# Index

**A**

accountability, 177
affected people. *See* nondominant group members
affinity bias, 145
Alcoff, Linda Martín, 76
allyship, 127–49
    active vs. passive forms of, 128–29
    champion/assistant dilemma, 130–32
    defined, 11
    impact of, 127–28
    motivation and, 13, 134–35, 178
    offering help, 135–39
    Platinum Rule and, 131–32, 137, 142, 146, 148, 152
    rotating nature of, 11, 154–55
    savior mentality and, 132–34
    systemic solutions, 144–47
    types of help, 139–43
    unconscious bias and, 143–44
    *See also* generosity to the source
Amram, Megan, 121–22

Anderson, Carol, 93, 94
Anderson, Ryan, 86–87
anger, 35–36, 51, 53
Annunzio, Susan Lucia, 167–68
Antony, Louise, 79
apology, 105–25
    ambivalent, 107
    growth vs. fixed mindsets and, 122–24
    healing effects of, 107
    rarity of, 106
    recognition and, 108–10
    redress and, 119–22
    remorse and, 116–18
    responsibility and, 110–16
"attack" conversational trap, 29–31
Atwood, Margaret, 90
"avoid" conversational trap, 16–20
Azaria, Hank, 118

**B**

Banaji, Mahzarin, 144
Barr, Roseanne, 110–11
Batali, Mario, 117

beginner's bubble, 72–73
"best friends" deflection, 24
bias, ubiquity of, 46–48
blanket immunity, 109
Bohnet, Iris, 144, 145, 146
Bolling, Eric, 16–17
Boyle, Rachel, 31
Brown, Brené, 158
Brown, Hannah, 115–16
Brown-Grooms, Brenda, 92
butpology, 111–13, 117
Bynum, G. T., 159–60

**C**

calling in. *See* generosity to the
    source
cancel culture, 90–91
Cannon, Nick, 120–21
champion/assistant dilemma,
    130–32
Chan, Jordan, 127
channel switching, 22–24
check-mark rule, 145
Chu, Arthur, 114
Chu, Charles, 134
Chugh, Dolly, 160–61
Cochran, Gennica, 127–29, 136
Cohen, Geoffrey, 42
comfort ring theory, 54–59, 117–18
commonalities
    misplaced empathy and, 3,
        25–26
    uncommon, 89–94
controversy scale, 86–89
conversational traps (A.D.D.A.),
    15–33
    attack, 29–31
    avoid, 16–20
    deflect, 20–26, 58
    deny, 26–29
    resilience as solution to, 38
    ubiquity of, 16
cookie seeking, 134
Cooper, Abraham, 121
Cooper, Amy, 166–67

Cooper, Christian, 166–67
Covey, Stephen, 119
Crenshaw, Kimberlé, 22
Crutcher, Terence, 159–60
crying, 54–57
curiosity, 61–82
    allyship and, 142
    generosity to the source and,
        155–56
    headwinds/tailwinds asymmetry
        and, 63–65
    increasing knowledge and, 66–71,
        80–81
    learning posture and, 70–75
    listening and, 74–75
    need for, 61–63
    overconfidence and, 61–62,
        72–73
    testimonial injustice and,
        75–80

**D**

Damore, James, 98, 99
*Dare to Speak* (Nossel), 102
Davidai, Shai, 63–64
"deflect" conversational trap, 20–26,
    58
DeGeneres, Ellen, 108–9
democratization of discomfort, 4–5,
    37–38
Dennett, Daniel, 90
"deny" conversational trap, 26–29
DiAngelo, Robin, 57
differences, ignoring, 18–19
disagreement. *See* respectful
    disagreement
discomfort
    democratization of, 4–5, 37–38
    labeling, 48–54
dominant groups. *See* privilege
Dotson, Kristie, 73
downswitching, 23
"dump out" rule. *See* ring theory
Dunn, Andy, 6
Dweck, Carol, 38–39, 158

**E**

Eddo-Lodge, Reni, 44, 78
Edmondson, Amy, 161
elderspeak, 139–40
Ely, Robin, 18
emotional reactions, 49–54
    anger, 35–36, 51, *53*
    examples, 35–37
    fear, 50–51, *53*
    guilt, 36–37, 51–52, *53*
    hopelessness, 52, *53*
    naming, 49–50, 52–54, *53*
empathy, misplaced, 3, 25–26
Evans, Ieshia, 140
expectations, managing, 96–97

**F**

Fabello, Melissa, 19
Fair, Caitlin Deen, 131
fauxpology, 116–17
Favreau, Jon, 5
fear, 5–6, 50–51, 53
feedback, right-size, 43–49, 58, 160
Feldblum, Chai, 41–42
Fey, Tina, 122–24
Findlay, Carly, 19
fixed vs. growth mindsets. *See* growth
    vs. fixed mindsets
Floyd, George, 141
Fortgang, Tal, 45
Fox, Laurence, 30–31
Fricker, Miranda, 76, 79

**G**

generational divides, 6, 47–48
generosity to the source, 151–71
    admitting mistakes and, 160–63
    curiosity and, 155–56
    opting out of, 166–69
    reflexive condemnation and,
        151–52
    resistance to, 153–54
    rotating nature of allyship and,
        154–55
    scripts for, 164–66

    separating person from behavior,
        156–60
Gilbert, Sara, 111
Gillis, Shane, 117
Gilovich, Thomas, 63–64
Glasgow, Bart, 93–94
Glasgow, Coley, 93–94
Goldman, Barry, 54–55
Goodman, Diane, 17
Greenwald, Anthony, 144
Groening, Matt, 28, 118
growth vs. fixed mindsets
    apology and, 122–24
    *The Magical Yet* and, 38, 41
    resilience and, 38–42, 58–59
    responsibility and, 115
    self-talk and, 41–42
    separating person from behavior
        and, 158
guilt, 36–37, 51–52, *53*, 158

**H**

Hamad, Ruby, 56
Hamburger, David, 119–20
hard-knock life effect, 25, 58
Hart, Kevin, 28–29
Hathaway, Anne, 110
Hayes, Chris, 156
Headlee, Celeste, 46–47
headwinds/tailwinds asymmetry,
    63–65
Heen, Sheila, 43–44
Herrnstein, Richard, 88
"Holier Than Me?" (Monin), 161–62
Holmes, Oliver Wendell, 113
hooks, bell, 156
hopelessness, 52, *53*
Howes, Molly, 107, 120
Hughey, Matthew, 132–33
humility, 75

**I**

identity conversations
    defined, 10
    difficulty of, 3–6, 32

identity conversations (*cont.*)
    emotional reactions to, 35–37,
        49–54
    inadequate guidance for, 8–9
    inescapability of, 6–8
    positive examples, 173–75
    practicing, 176
    tensions between strategies,
        175–76
ifpology, 108–10, 117
*Inside Out*, 49
intentions
    responsibility and, 113–14
    self-deflection and, 26
    separating person from behavior
        and, 158–59
intersectionality, 22, 45
Isay, Dave, 92
"I" statements, 74

**J**
Jack, Anthony Abraham, 146
Jaigirdar, Adiba, 56
Jarrett, Valerie, 111
Jenner, Kendall, 140
*Just Ask!* (Sotomayor), 138

**K**
Kador, John, 107
Kahneman, Daniel, 72
Katz, Mitch, 23
Kelly, Megyn, 27
Kennedy, John, 47
King, Bernice, 140
knowledge sources, 66–70
    nondominant group members as,
        67–70, 80–81
    overload and, 67–68
    public sources, 66–67
Kondabolu, Hari, 28

**L**
Lazare, Aaron, 106
learning posture, 70–75
Lee, Harper, 132–33

legal arena, 1–2
Lerner, Harriet, 107, 109–10
Letterman, David, 123
Lipman, Joanne, 37, 50–51
listening, 74–75
Livingston, Ed, 23
Livingston, Robert, 43, 72
Lofthouse, Michael, 127–28
Loubriel, Jennifer, 57
Lowery, Brian, 25

**M**
Mack, Corine, 119
Madonna, 114
*The Magical Yet*, 38, 41
Maitlis, Emily, 17
Marans, Noam, 121
Markle, Meghan, 30–31
#MeToo movement, 51, 154
misgendering, 4
misplaced empathy, 3, 25–26
mistakes, admitting, 160–63
Monin, Benoît, 161–62
Moodie-Mills, Aisha, 17
Morelock, Judy, 51
motivation for allyship, 13, 134–35,
    178
Mounk, Yascha, 5
multidimensional nature of privilege,
    45
Munroe, Randall, 97
Murray, Charles, 88
Myers, Vernā, 51–52

**N**
naming emotional reactions, 49–50,
    52–54, *53*
Narayan, Uma, 67
Neff, Kristin, 52
Neville, Phil, 114–15
Noah, Trevor, 27–28, 68
Nolan, Savala, 18
nondominant group members
    as knowledge sources, 67–70, 80–81
    discomfort for, 4–5, 37–38

frustration of, 4, 63
impact of ignoring differences on, 18–19
impact of silence on, 18
impact of skepticism commentary on, 78
knowledge gaps and, 64–65
new language and, 6–7
offers of help and, 135–39
overload and, 67–68
privacy and, 69
ring theory and, 56–57
testimonial injustice and, 75–77
tone policing of, 20–21
universalization and, 67
Norton, Jim, 28
Nossel, Suzanne, 102

**O**
off-ramps, 20, 38, 54, 97
Oluo, Ijeoma, 30, 47, 67
Orman, Suze, 86–87
Osbourne, Kelly, 26
overload, 67–68

**P**
Padman, Monica, 118
Parker, Kayla, 51
Peters, Benno, 141, 142
Phelps-Roper, Megan, 168
Phillips, L. Taylor, 25
Pinker, Steven, 90
Platinum Rule, 131–32, 137, 142, 146, 148, 152
Plous, Scott, 160
political activism, 168–69
Ponsetto, Miya, 109
practice, 176
*Predator* handshake meme, 89
privacy
champion/assistant dilemma and, 130–31
controversy scale and, 88

headwinds/tailwinds asymmetry, 63–65
multidimensional nature of, 45
rarity of apologizing and, 106
right-size feedback and, 44–46
self-deflection and, 25
testimonial injustice and, 77
Professor Griff, 120
psychological safety, 161
Puckey, Andrew, 113–14

**R**
Rancic, Giuliana, 70, 75
recognition, 108–10
redress, 119–22
reflective mode, 79
reflexive condemnation, 151–52
reframing, 52–54, *53*
Reinhart, Lili, 140–41
remorse, 116–18
resilience, 35–60
emotional reactions and, 35–37, 49–54
growth mindset and, 38–42, 58–59
right-size feedback and, 44–49, 58
ring theory and, 54–59, 117–18
self-affirmation and, 42–43
respectful disagreement, 83–104
allyship and, 143
controversy scale and, 86–89
vs. fauxpology, 117
managing expectations and, 96–97
possibility of, 102–3
showing your work and, 94–96
social context and, 98–101
uncommon commonalities and, 89–94
responsibility, 110–16

Richeson, Jennifer, 4
right-size feedback, 43–49, 58, 160
ring theory, 54–59, 117–18, 142
Roberts, Shoshana, 61–62
Ross, Loretta, 169–70
Rumsfeld, Donald, 71
running commentary of skepticism, 77–80

**S**

Saad, Layla, 21
Santagati, Steve, 61–62, 72
savior mentality, 132–34
Seales, Amanda, 61–62
self-affirmation, 42–43
self-comparisons, 41
self-deflection conversational trap, 24–26, 58
self-disclosure, 160–63
self-image, 159–60
self-talk, 41–42, 77–78
shame, 12–13, 158, 177
Shearer, Harry, 108
Shen, Wenny, 146
Sherman, David, 42
showing your work, 94–96
Sia, 29–30
silence, 18
Silk, Susan, 54–55
Simms, David, 115
Sinclair, Upton, 77
skepticism, running commentary of, 77–80
"Smalley, Stuart," 42
*Snyder v. Phelps*, 156–57, 168
social media
    difficulty of identity conversations and, 5
    unhelpful help and, 141
Sorkin, Aaron, 135
Sotomayor, Sonia, 138
Spencer, Richard, 98
Steinem, Gloria, 90
Stevenson, Bryan, 158

Stone, Douglas, 43–44
support, appropriate, 54–58

**T**

talkpology, 119–20
Tatum, Beverly Daniel, 47
Taylor, Breonna, 141
technology, 5
testimonial injustice, 75–80
"Thank you, because . . . ," 92
*Thinking, Fast and Slow* (Kahneman), 72
*30 Rock*, 123
third-man rule, 146
Thomas, David, 18
*To Kill a Mockingbird* (Lee), 132–33, 135
tone policing, 20–21
Tran, Kim, 129
Tsuneta, Alexandra, 18
20/60/20 rule, 167–68
two-two rule, 145

**U**

*Unbreakable Kimmy Schmidt, The*, 122
unhelpful help, 139–45
Unice, Nicole, 92
universalization, 67
unknown unknowns, 71–72, 80–81
upswitching, 23, 113–14
Utt, Jamie, 113

**V**

V (Eve Ensler), 105–6, 108–9
Venn diagrams, 89–90
virtue signaling, 134
Volokh, Sasha, 156–57

**W**

wait-five-seconds rule, 146
Walsh, Matt, 44–45
Wang, Katie, 139
Warren, Elizabeth, 129

Weigel, Moira, 96
Westboro Baptist Church, 156–57, 168
white savior mentality, 132–34
white supremacy culture, 8–9
Whitfield, Fredricka, 61–62
Williams, Schele, 10
*Witches, The*, 110

**Y**
Yoffe, Emily, 5
Young, Damon, 67–68

**Z**
Zendaya, 70–71
Zhao, Xuan, 92
Zheng, Lily, 48–49, 117

# About the Authors

**Kenji Yoshino** is the Chief Justice Earl Warren professor of Constitutional Law at NYU School of Law and the faculty director of the Meltzer Center for Diversity, Inclusion, and Belonging. Kenji studied at Harvard, Oxford, and Yale Law School. His fields are constitutional law, antidiscrimination law, and law and literature. He has received several distinctions for his teaching and research, including the American Bar Association's Silver Gavel Award, the Peck Medal in Jurisprudence, and New York University's Distinguished Teaching Award. Kenji is the author of three books—*Covering: The Hidden Assault on Our Civil Rights*; *A Thousand Times More Fair: What Shakespeare's Plays Teach Us About Justice*; and *Speak Now: Marriage Equality on Trial*. He has published in major academic journals, including the *Harvard Law Review*, the *Stanford Law Review*, and the *Yale Law Journal*, as well as popular venues such as the *Los Angeles Times*, the *New York Times*, and the *Washington Post*. He serves on the board of the Brennan Center for Justice, advisory boards for diversity and inclusion at Charter Communications and Morgan Stanley, and on the board of his children's school.

**David Glasgow** is the executive director of the Meltzer Center for Diversity, Inclusion, and Belonging and an adjunct professor at NYU School of Law. He graduated with a BA in philosophy and an LLB (first class honors) from the University of Melbourne, Australia, and clerked on the Federal Court of Australia. A dual-qualified attorney in New York and Australia, he practiced employment, labor relations, and antidiscrimination law at law firm King & Wood Mallesons before completing his master of laws (LLM) degree in 2014 at NYU School of Law, where he was awarded the David H. Moses Memorial Prize and the George Colin Award. He has written for a range of publications including the *Harvard Business Review, HuffPost,* and *Slate,* and served as an associate director of the Public Interest Law Center at NYU School of Law prior to his current role.

# Reading Group Guide

These questions are intended for book clubs, educational institutions, and workplaces that wish to host small-group discussions around the content of *Say the Right Thing*.

1. Early in the introduction, the authors offer four examples of identity conversations—a white male leader trying to display empathy at a company forum on race, a woman who shushes her toddler son at a grocery store for commenting on a baby's medical condition, a boomer uncle who defends himself after he's told to stop commenting on a woman's attractiveness, and a student who over-apologizes for using the wrong gender pronoun to refer to a transgender student. Could you imagine yourself in situations like these, and if so, how would you handle them?

2. The authors argue that an "age-based divide" has opened in the approach people take to conversations about identity. Have you noticed a difference in how these

conversations unfold when you're speaking across generations? If so, how?

**3.** In Principle 1 (Beware the Four Conversational Traps), the authors introduce an example of Amir, a friend who doesn't attend your annual holiday parties because the gatherings are racially homogeneous. Could you imagine yourself on the more privileged side of a conversation like this one (on race or any other grounds)? If so, how do you think you would respond to a statement like Amir's?

**4.** Do you think the categories of "avoid," "deflect," "deny," and "attack" described in Principle 1 (Beware the Four Conversational Traps) cover the major types of undesirable ally behavior in identity conversations? Did any of the examples that the authors provide under these headings particularly resonate with you (or fail to resonate)?

**5.** In Principle 2 (Build Resilience), the authors observe that identity conversations can prompt extreme emotional discomfort, which often takes the form of fear, anger, guilt, or hopelessness. When you have identity conversations in your own life, what emotions do you typically feel? Do those emotions lead you to behave in a particular way when having these dialogues?

**6.** In Principle 2 (Build Resilience), the authors provide five strategies for managing your emotional discomfort—adopt a growth mindset, self-affirm, right-size feedback, name and reframe your discomfort, and seek appropriate support using "ring theory." Can you imagine yourself using any of these strategies before, during, or after a conversation about identity? How would you implement them?

**7.** In Principle 3 (Cultivate Curiosity), the authors encourage you to teach yourself about identity issues. In what areas of identity (e.g., race, ethnicity, gender, sexual orientation, gender identity, disability, age, religion) do you currently feel that you lack knowledge? How would you go about closing that knowledge gap?

**8.** What experiences have you had (good or bad) when disagreeing with someone on an identity issue? Does the authors' distinction in Principle 4 (Disagree Respectfully) among "green," "yellow," and "red" disagreements help you think about how and when to communicate your disagreements on these topics?

**9.** Have you ever given or received an apology on an issue of identity? How did it go? Did you (or the other person) follow the four elements outlined in Principle 5 (Apologize Authentically) of recognition, responsibility, remorse, and redress?

**10.** In Principle 6 (Apply the Platinum Rule), the authors open with examples of allies who did and didn't intervene when they witnessed non-inclusive behavior— Gennica Cochran, who stepped in to challenge a man who spewed racist abuse in a restaurant, and attendees at a family gathering who failed to intervene when someone referred to COVID-19 as "the China virus." Think back to a time when you observed non-inclusive behavior. How did you respond? If you didn't intervene, why not? If you did intervene, what did you say and how did the conversation unfold?

**11.** In Principle 7 (Be Generous to the Source), the authors encourage you to adopt "go-to phrases" you can use when you wish to confront a source of non-inclusive behavior. Do you currently have a go-to phrase? If not, what words could you imagine saying that are authentic to you?

12. Throughout the book, the authors use anecdotes from their own experiences or from the public sphere. Were there any examples where you disagreed with the authors' discussion of the issue? If so, how would you have analyzed it differently?

13. Some critics argue that teaching people what to say (and not to say) in identity conversations will lead to greater anxiety and turn natural human interactions into minefields. What do you make of that critique? Do you feel more anxious or less anxious about identity conversations after having read this book? To the extent you feel more anxious, is that necessarily a bad outcome?

14. What's one thing you'll do differently in conversations about identity, diversity, and justice now that you've read this book?